Bedrooms
for COOL KIDS

CREATIVE
PUBLISHING
international

CHANHASSEN, MINNESOTA
www.creativepub.com

Copyright © 2002
Creative Publishing international, Inc.
18705 Lake Drive East
Chanhassen, Minnesota 55317
1-800-328-3895
www.creativepub.com
All rights reserved
Printed in U.S.A.

President/CEO: Michael Eleftheriou
Vice President/Publisher: Linda Ball
Vice President/Retail Sales & Marketing: Kevin Haas

BEDROOMS FOR COOL KIDS
Created by: The Editors of
Creative Publishing international

Executive Editor: Elaine Perry
Managing Editor: Yen Le
Senior Editor: Linda Neubauer
Art Director: Megan Noller
Project & Prop Stylists: Christine Jahns,
    Joanne Wawra
Samplemakers: Arlene Dohrman, Sheila Duffy,
    Teresa Henn
Photo Stylists: Heidi Grayden, Joanne Wawra
Photographers: Tate Carlson, Charles Nields,
    Andrea Rugg
Scene Shop Carpenters: Scott Ashfeld, Christopher
    Neubauer, Dan Sommerfeld, Dan Widerski
Director of Production Services: Kim Gerber
Contributors: C.M. Offray and Son, Inc.,
    Fabric Traditions, HTC, Inc., Kirsch, Kunin Felt
    (Foss Manufacturing Company, Inc.)

ISBN 1-58923-050-7

Printed on American paper by:
R. R. Donnelley
10 9 8 7 6 5 4 3 2 1

Library of Congress Cataloging-in-Publication Data

Bedrooms for cool kids : clever ideas and practical plans for creating
imaginative spaces.
    p. cm.
    Includes index.
    ISBN 1-58923-050-7 (pbk.)
    1. Bedrooms--Remodeling--Amateurs' manuals.
    I. Creative Publishing International.
    TH4816.3.B43 B43 2002
    747.7'7--dc21
                                2002017370

Creative Publishing international, Inc. offers
a variety of how-to books. For information write:
    Creative Publishing international, Inc.
     Subscriber Books
    18705 Lake Drive East
    Chanhassen, MN 55317

Contents

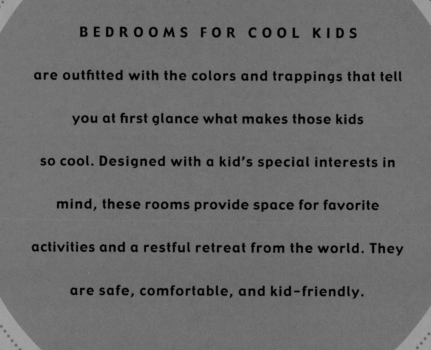

BEDROOMS FOR COOL KIDS

are outfitted with the colors and trappings that tell

you at first glance what makes those kids

so cool. Designed with a kid's special interests in

mind, these rooms provide space for favorite

activities and a restful retreat from the world. They

are safe, comfortable, and kid-friendly.

A cool kid's bedroom also has lots of convenient storage. We parents appreciate that because we have an affinity for neatness. And we believe that kids, whether they admit it or not, like to keep their things in order because it builds their sense of ownership. Or is it that they *will* keep their things in order *if* they feel a sense of ownership for their room?

Ownership is a crucial thing when it comes to a bedroom. Kids spend a lot of time in their rooms, and their rooms should be a reflection of themselves. So, it's important to ask our kids for advice and suggestions before we rearrange and decorate their personal space. What are their favorite colors? What are their favorite pastimes? Who are their heroes? What are their fears? Would they rather dance or play hockey; draw pictures or play video games? What do they want their rooms to look like? Kids have some pretty imaginative ideas about decorating. Of course, we get to incorporate some of their wild ideas into more practical solutions and make final decisions that

fit our budget and time. But kids' feedback is vital to designing bedrooms that really fit them.

In *Bedrooms for Cool Kids,* we have designed five theme bedrooms, each one fitting the personality and interests

of a particularly cool kid between the ages of four and ten. These are not high-budget decorator's dream bedrooms, filled with adult ideas of what kids should like. They are affordable, sensible, and realistic rooms that you can create for your own cool kids,

with money left over for music lessons, braces, and college.

Each room concept includes complete plans for transforming an average-size bedroom into a magical haven. We have created painted walls, bedding ensembles, and easy window treatments that play leading roles in establishing the themes. The colorful supporting cast includes unique storage ideas and lots of easy-to-make room accessories. Most importantly, everything is geared to work with and encourage a kid's imagination.

Whether you are a complete do-it-yourselfer or have the time and skills to tackle only a few of the projects, the directions and ideas here will help you create a room that fits your one-of-a-kind kid. If the two of you decide on a different room theme, there are countless ideas here that can be easily adapted. You are sure to find personal satisfaction in the creative process alone. But the real reward will be the delight and enthusiasm you see as that cool kid of yours settles into a newly decorated bedroom that fits perfectly.

CHOOSING COLORS

Kids love bold colors, and they want to be surrounded by all of their favorites. A child's favorite hues may be pretty apparent by the clothes he or she loves to wear or by the colors that are worn down the fastest in the crayon box. Of course, a kid's absolute favorite colors today may be rejected tomorrow. Adults love color, too, but we tend to want smaller, more subtle doses, in design-savvy

ABOVE:
Traffic sign pillows
(page 74) accent a
motorhead's haven
with bold graphics
and bright colors.

schemes that we can live with for a while. In decorating a kid's bedroom, the trick is to satisfy his or her thirst for color without creating a parent-repelling environment.

Color favorites, even the unusual ones, can be used in small, easily changeable ways. Paint gives you unlimited options. Since repainting the walls on a kid's every whim is out of the question, it's smart to let the walls serve as a subtle backdrop and reserve the bolder colors for room accents. Occasional color changes of smaller surfaces like drawer fronts, knobs, lamp shades, bookends, wall shelves, or a chair rail are more feasible. Fabrics provide lots of color options, too. Bold color requests can be satisfied in throw pillows, window valances, or small rugs that can be added or changed less expensively than a bedspread or draperies.

Colors influence our emotions, behaviors, and perceptions. Cool colors (blues, greens, and aquas) have a serene, calming effect, perhaps beneficial for a child who is hyperactive or who has difficulty winding down for bedtime. These colors also have

the power to visually expand space, making them good options for the walls of a small bedroom. Warm colors (reds, oranges, and yellows) have an energizing effect, possibly helpful for a shy or overly cautious child. Visually advancing, warm colors have the power to create coziness in an otherwise large room.

Wall colors, because they represent the largest space proportion in the room, will have the most influence in the color scheme. It is wise to purchase only a small amount of the desired color and paint it on a large sheet of tagboard as a trial. Hang it on the wall and view it at various times under different lighting conditions to determine if the color is right for you and your child. Notice that incandescent lightbulbs, most often used in bedrooms, give off a yellow cast that tends to turn blues slightly gray and intensifies oranges, yellows, and reds. If your choice is a warm color, select a lighter shade than your first impulse. For blues and greens, select clear colors that can hold their own in low daylight and artificial lighting.

THE COLOR WHEEL

The color wheel conveniently organizes colors, making it easier to select a scheme. PRIMARY colors—red, yellow, and blue—are the source of all other colors. They are located equal distances apart on the wheel. SECONDARY colors—green, violet, and orange—are located halfway between the primary colors from which they are made. TERTIARY or intermediate colors are formed from the combination of a primary and a secondary color. Colors that are directly opposite each other on the wheel are called COMPLEMENTARY. Neighboring colors are referred to as ANALOGOUS.

The wheel shows the PURE colors, which are considerably bold. White is added to pure colors to make TINTS, familiar as the pastel palette. Black is added to pure colors to make darker SHADES of them. Complementary color is added to a pure color to create a sophisticated, subdued COMPLEMENT TINT or TONE. Children generally prefer the pure colors or tints. When combined with white accents, whether in the furniture or other accessories, these colors are even more striking.

The color wheel is helpful for developing aesthetically pleasing color schemes. MONOCHROMATIC schemes are made up of tints, shades, and tones of the same color. ANALOGOUS schemes include colors that are adjacent to each other on the color wheel, and may include various tints, shades, or tones of each. COMPLEMENTARY schemes use two colors from opposite sides of the wheel. For best results, one color is used predominantly and the other is used as an accent. SPLIT COMPLEMENTARY schemes combine one color with the two colors that are next to its complement. TRIADS use three colors equidistant on the wheel, such as red, blue, and yellow, or their pastel counterparts, both kid's room favorites.

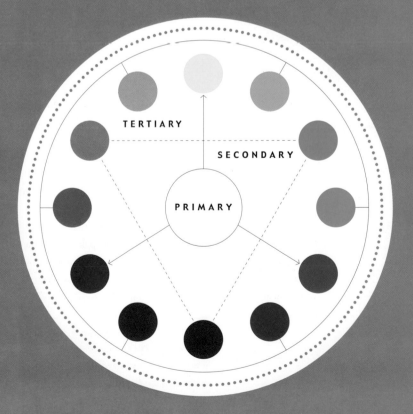

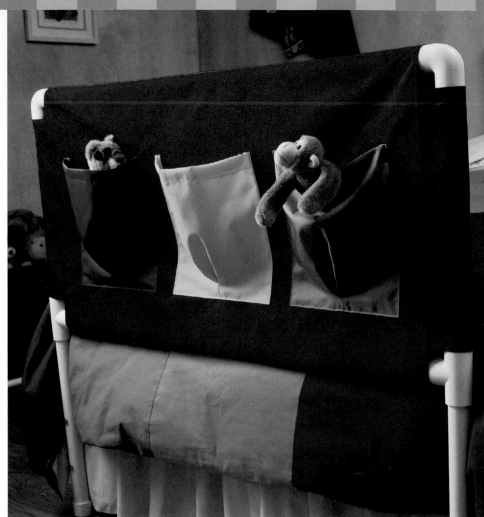

ABOVE:
Lively paint colors
and clever drawer
knobs give
plain furniture
cool-kid appeal.

FURNITURE & STORAGE

The largest share of your decorating budget will be spent on the furniture, so make some plans before you buy. Try to plan a few years down the road. Some furniture pieces are versatile enough to be used in different ways as your child grows. Unpainted furniture, usually less expensive than finished pieces, allows you to get creative with colors and room themes without sacrificing quality. There is also the option of buying inexpensive, paintable, juvenile furniture that will probably last as long as one or two children in the family are small enough to use it.

The bed heads the list, of course. While we have shown single beds in the rooms we have designed, other options include larger sizes, trundles, and bunks. If room size permits,

options that provide room for occasional sleepover guests or siblings are a good investment. Most teenagers are not comfortable in a single bed, so unless you plan to pass a smaller bed down to a sibling, don't pay top dollar for a single bed that your child will outgrow in a few years. While headboards and footboards are not essential, they can be designed to emphasize the room theme and even provide storage.

Another essential piece of furniture is a chest of drawers. Even if the closet is large enough for storing all the clothes, a chest of drawers is useful for storing other items, like games, art supplies, and puzzles. Its top provides a surface for lamps, picture frames, books between bookends, and other personal items.

Armoires are very versatile. They can be outfitted for different purposes from infancy to adulthood. During the grade-school years, an armoire could become a game and toy storage cabinet, an artist's corner, an entertainment center, or even a study nook. In this case, paying for quality the first time will ensure its usefulness for many years.

A nightstand, especially one with some drawer space, is useful for bedside storage, for supporting lamps and clocks, and for keeping other personal items close at hand. A storage crate or low bookshelf placed alongside the bed would work as well.

If the bedroom is also the playroom and study room, it is important to include a kid-size table and chairs or a small desk. A space for drawing, coloring, and writing can be created with a smooth board placed over wire storage units or wooden crates.

Bookcases, shelves, and hook racks are ideal for storing and displaying collections, trophies, books, and other kid paraphernalia. Unique shelving and hook ideas accompany each of the themed bedrooms. Besides helping organize the room, they provide a sense of identity and ownership, especially when they are kid-friendly and placed at kid-height.

LIGHTING

Kids' bedrooms should include both ambient and task lighting. Ambient lighting, whether a fixture in the center of the ceiling, track lighting, or recessed lighting, provides general illumination for the entire room. Avoid fixtures that distort the light or create odd shadowing effects. Ceiling fan lights are a good idea. The blades can be painted to fit the decorating scheme, while providing gentle airflow. Task lighting may include a small lamp placed by the bedside for nighttime reading or on a desk for doing homework. Home centers and specialty lighting stores provide kits and parts for making your own lamps, allowing you to use creative task lighting to accent the bedroom decorating theme.

FLOOR PLANS

Kids' bedrooms never seem to have enough space, and a poor room arrangement can eat up even more. Start your decorating plan by laying the room out to scale on the graph provided on page 15. Include the entry door, closet doors, windows, and any built-in features. Note the distance from the bottom of the windows to the floor; also note the location of heat and cold air return vents, phone jacks, and electrical outlets and switches. Trace and cut out the scale-size furniture pieces you are considering, and try some different room arrangements, following the general guidelines provided.

Between the ages of four and ten, kids use their rooms for a variety of activities: sleeping, studying, reading, creating artwork, practicing an instrument, playing make believe, and entertaining friends. If possible, designate areas in the room where one or more of these activities can take place, and arrange the furniture to accommodate your plan.

Begin by positioning the bed, since it requires the most room. If you still have to acquire the bed, working up this room plan will help you decide what size you can buy. If you anticipate storage will be a problem, you may want to consider a bed with built-in drawers or at least one with room for under-bed storage boxes. Place the bed where it won't block the

door or any vents, and preferably not under a window. In small bedrooms, placing the head and one side of the bed against adjoining walls is usually the most space-efficient placement. Against a wall, the bed also will not block the traffic flow in the room.

Assuming the bed will also become a favorite area for reading, a nightstand and lamp should go next to the bed. Ideally, this would mean that an electrical outlet is nearby. A small

FLOOR PLAN: Flower Garden Fantasy Room

STORAGE

CHAIR

TABLE

STORAGE

RUG

CHAIR

TWIN BED

RUG

CHEST

RUG

NIGHTSTAND

STORAGE

CLOSET

GRID:
1 Square = 1'
(30.5 cm)

LEFT: The layout of the flower garden fantasy room (page 17) includes areas for play and rest with open spaces for dancing.

bookcase can be substituted for a nightstand. A bookcase headboard is an option that could eliminate the need for a nightstand.

Play areas for younger kids may give way to study areas for older kids, so think about the future. Both activities require a work surface and storage, whether it is for toys, games, and artwork or school books, crafting supplies, and desk accessories. You may include a small table and chairs for a younger

child, replacing it with a desk when the child gets older. Avoid splitting up the necessary storage for this area with another part of the room. The area is more likely to stay picked up and neat if shelves, bins, or toy chests are within easy reach.

Leave as much free space as possible. Allow 36" (91.5 cm) at the foot of the bed and between the bed and any doors that open into the room. Also allow 36" (91.5 cm) in front of the closet. In front

of furniture with drawers, allow enough space to comfortably stand with the drawers open. Also, leave room behind any chairs for pulling them out to sit or stand.

When you have determined the furniture arrangement that meets your criteria, sketch elevation drawings of each wall, so you will know how the pieces look. This will also help you determine where open wall space can be used for bulletin boards, artwork displays, shelves, or maps.

FURNITURE TEMPLATES: Nightstand, Bed, Chest, Bookcase, Armoire, Desk, Table, Storage, & Chair

NIGHT
STAND:
28" × 18"
(71 × 46 cm)

NIGHT
STAND:
24" × 20"
(61 × 51 cm)

NIGHT
STAND:
24" × 16"
(61 × 40.5 cm)

NIGHT
STAND:
20" × 14"
(51 × 35.5 cm)

NIGHT
STAND:
16" × 19"
(40.5 ×
48.5 cm)

NIGHT
STAND:
16" × 16"
(40.5 ×
40.5 cm)

TWIN BED
WITH
HEADBOARD:
44" × 75"
(112 × 190.5 cm)

MATTRESS:
39" × 75"
(99 × 190.5 cm)

DOUBLE BED
WITH
HEADBOARD:
59" × 75"
(149.8 × 190.5 cm)

MATTRESS:
54" × 75"
(137 × 190.5 cm)

CHEST:
48" × 21" × 36"
(122 × 53.5 × 91.5 cm)

CHEST:
42" × 21" × 44"
(107 × 53.5 × 112 cm)

BOOKCASE:
48" × 12"
(122 × 30.5 cm)

BOOKCASE:
36" × 12"
(91.5 × 30.5 cm)

CHEST:
48" × 16" × 36"
(122 × 40.5 × 91.5 cm)

CHEST:
30" × 21" × 36"
(76 × 53.5 × 91.5 cm)

BOOKCASE:
60" × 12"
(152.5 × 30.5 cm)

BOOKCASE:
30" × 12"
(76 × 30.5 cm)

ARMOIRE:
42" × 24"
(107 × 61 cm)

ARMOIRE:
38" × 21"
(96.5 × 53.5 cm)

CHEST:
36" × 16" × 36"
(91.5 × 40.5 × 91.5 cm)

CHEST:
30" × 16" × 36"
(76 × 40.5 × 91.5 cm)

DESK:
50" × 25"
(127 × 63.5 cm)

DESK:
40" × 18"
(102 × 46 cm)

TABLE:
30" × 30"
(76 × 76 cm)

TABLE:
20" × 20"
(51 × 51 cm)

TABLE:
24"
(61 cm)

TABLE:
18"
(46 cm)

STORAGE:
48" × 16"
(122 × 40.5 cm)

STORAGE:
36" × 19"
(91.5 × 48.5 cm)

STORAGE:
26" × 16"
(66 × 40.5 cm)

STORAGE:
19" × 19"
(48.5 ×
48.5 cm)

CHAIR:
13" × 14"
(33 ×
35.5 cm)

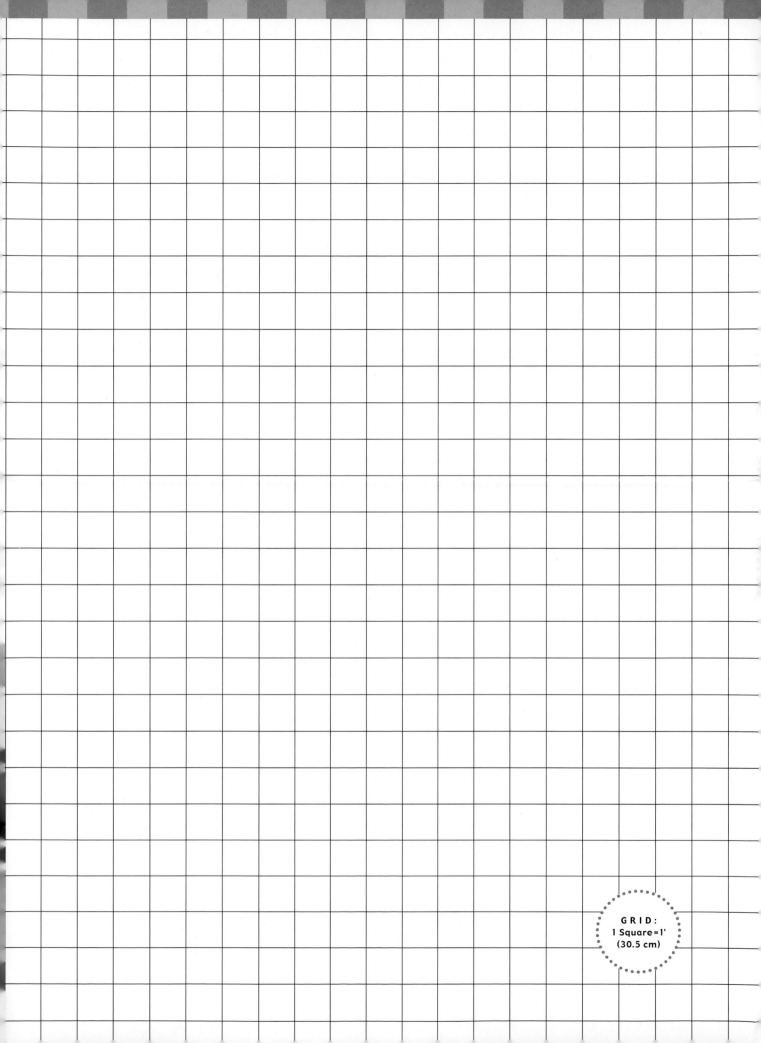

GRID:
1 Square=1'
(30.5 cm)

Flower

CHILDHOOD IS ONE BIG BED OF roses, at least in this little girl's secret bedroom garden. Here her dreams unfold like the blossoms that surround her and take flight with the friendly bugs that share her space. Clever and efficient use of gardeners' paraphernalia gives her bedroom a charming, almost whimsical, character. What a delight to wake up every morning in such a pretty bedroom!

Garden Fantasy

Picket Fence Wall

The bedroom becomes a fenced-in flower garden with a perky picket fence painted on the wall. Simple masking techniques help you complete the job quickly.

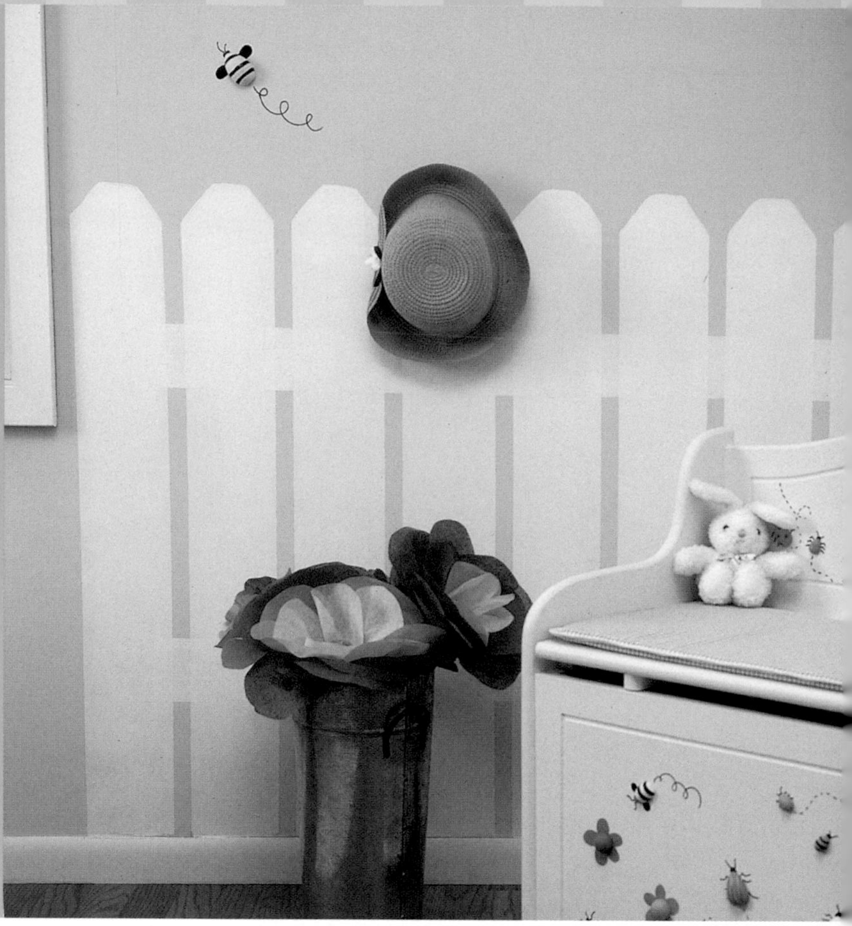

MATERIALS

- Latex satin-finish paint in base coat color
- Latex satin-finish paint in fence color
- Painter's masking tape, 1" (2.5 cm) wide
- Heavy paper for pattern

TOOLS

- 9" (23 cm) roller cage and 2 roller covers; paint tray
- Carpenter's level
- Straightedge
- 1" (2.5 cm) paintbrush or foam applicator
- 4" (10 cm) roller cage and roller cover

HOW TO PAINT A PICKET FENCE WALL

1

Paint the entire wall the base coat color, using the large roller. Allow to dry thoroughly.

2

Using a carpenter's level and straightedge, draw a light pencil line on the wall 38" (96.5 cm) from the floor. Mark every 6" (15 cm) along the line. Mark every 6" (15 cm) just above the baseboard. Apply a vertical line of masking tape at each mark, extending 2" (5 cm) above the line.

3

Draw a pattern for fence board top 5" (12.7 cm) wide, creating an arch or a point, as desired. Lightly mark the board tops between tape edges and above marked line.

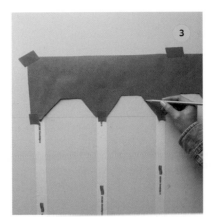

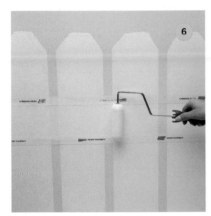

4

Paint the board tops, using a small
paintbrush or foam applicator. Paint the
rest of the boards, using a roller. Allow
to dry; remove masking tape.

5

Apply a line of masking tape 8" (20.5 cm)
below the top of the boards; apply a second
line 3½" (9 cm) below the first. Repeat
at the bottom of the fence, placing one row
8" (20.5 cm) above the baseboard and
a second row 3½" (9 cm) above the first.

6

Apply paint between the taped lines,
using a 4" (10 cm) paint roller. Allow to
dry; remove masking tape.

TRELLIS HOOK STANDS
& FLOWERPOT STORAGE

**Flower trellises become supports for hooks, offering a
place to hang fashion accessories and playthings.
Large plastic flowerpots provide handy places to
store stuffed animals, dolls, toys, and games.**

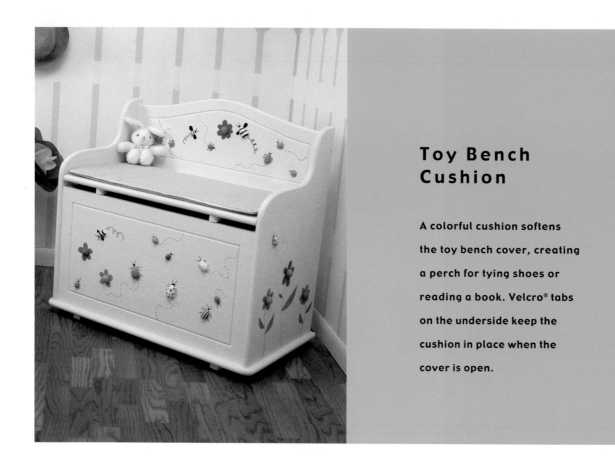

Toy Bench Cushion

A colorful cushion softens the toy bench cover, creating a perch for tying shoes or reading a book. Velcro® tabs on the underside keep the cushion in place when the cover is open.

HINT: A sturdy wooden toy box is a smart investment. It can be repainted when the child is older and used for storing almost anything. Look for one that has a safety space under the lid for preventing pinched fingers.

MATERIALS

- Fabric
- Underlining, optional
- ½" (1.3 cm) high-density polyurethane foam
- Four Velcro squares
- Velcro adhesive
- Extra-wide double-fold bias tape
- Glue stick
- Thread

TOOLS

- Sewing machine; zipper foot

HOW TO MAKE A CUSHION

1

Make a paper pattern of the toy bench seat, rounding sharp corners. Cut out the pattern; check the fit. Cut fabric for the front and back, using the pattern. Underline the pieces if the fabric is lightweight. Stitch the loop side of a Velcro square about 2" (5 cm) from each corner of the cushion back.

2

Mark a line ⅝" (1.5 cm) in from the outer edge of the pattern. Cut on the marked line. Cut a piece of foam, using this pattern.

3

Center the foam on the wrong side of the cushion back; place the cushion front over the foam, right side up, aligning fabric edges. Pin the layers together.

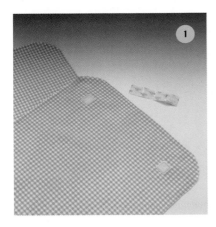

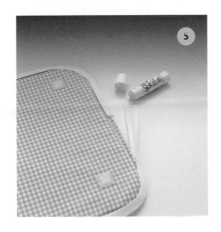

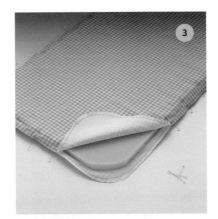

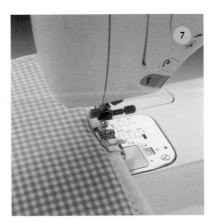

4

Machine-baste ¼" (6 mm) from edges around the cushion, using a zipper foot. Press the bias tape into a curved shape to match the outer edge of the cushion; stretch the tape slightly as you press.

5

Apply small amount of glue stick to seam allowance of cushion back. Finger-press the wide side of the bias tape into position, with the raw edges of the cushion at the foldline of the tape; overlap the ends 1" (2.5 cm).

6

Turn the cushion over. Glue-baste the narrow side of the tape to the seam allowance of the cushion front. Join the ends of the tape by turning under ¼" (6 mm) on the overlapped end.

7

Stitch along the inner edge of the tape, using the zipper foot, with the narrow side of tape facing up.

8

Place the cushion on the bench cover. Mark the locations of the Velcro squares. Adhere the hook side of the squares to the bench cover; allow to dry. Secure cushion to bench cover.

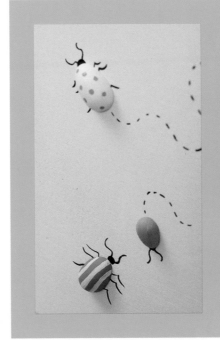

DIMENSIONAL BUGS

Wooden shapes give dimension to friendly bugs applied to the walls and furniture around the room. Look for half-egg shapes or those intended for specific bug bodies that can be painted with acrylic craft paints and glued in place. Then simply paint bug wings and legs on the flat surface around the shapes, using paint pens.

Garden Window Mirror

Imitating a garden window, this charming mirror is mounted at just the right height for your little girl. Hair ribbons, scrunchies, barrettes, and other grooming necessities are kept neatly at hand in little galvanized pails held in a window box below the mirror. A dainty gingham valance echoes the ones that hang above the real windows. If you purchase a mirror in a finished frame, omit steps 1 and 2, opposite.

MATERIALS

- 16" × 20" (40.5 × 51 cm) mirror mounted in a plain frame or mirror, frame, mat board, and glazing points
- Two swivel hangers
- $\frac{1}{3}$ yd. (0.32 m) fabric, 45" (115 cm) wide
- Thread
- Wooden dowel, $\frac{1}{4}$" (6 mm) in diameter
- Two screw hooks
- 1 × 4 pine board
- 15' (4.6 m) pine screen molding, $\frac{1}{4}$" × $\frac{3}{4}$" (6 mm × 2 cm)
- Wood glue
- 17 × $\frac{3}{4}$" (2 cm) brads
- Four small galvanized pails or clay pots, about 4" (10 cm) in diameter
- Glossy latex or acrylic craft paints
- Materials for making dimensional bugs (page 21), optional
- Two sawtooth hangers
- Rubber or cork bumpers

TOOLS

- Putty knife, optional
- Sewing machine
- Saw
- Sandpaper
- Drill; $\frac{1}{16}$" drill bit
- Hammer
- Screwdriver
- Paintbrush

HOW TO MAKE A WINDOW MIRROR

1

Sand, prime, and paint the picture frame. Cut a piece of mat board the same size as the mirror. Insert the mirror into the frame opening; cover the mirror back with the mat board.

2

Insert glazing points into the picture frame on all sides of the opening, pushing them into place with a putty knife.

3

Secure swivel hangers on sides of frame back, about one-third of the way down from the top, using screws; predrill the screw holes. Hang the mirror at the child's eye level.

4

Cut a full width of fabric for the valance, 12" (30.5 cm) long. Turn under and stitch a 1" (2.5 cm) double-fold bottom hem. If the selvages are neat, they can serve as side hems. If not, trim off selvages; turn under and stitch ½" (1.3 cm) double-fold side hems.

5

Press under ½" (1.3 cm) at the top. Then turn under 2" (5 cm); press. Stitch along the inner fold. Stitch again 1¼" (3.2 cm) from the outer fold, forming the rod pocket and heading.

6

Mark locations for screw hooks on the wall 3" (7.5 cm) above and 1" (2.5 cm) outside the mirror frame edges. Insert screw hooks.

7

Cut wooden dowel 2" (5 cm) longer than distance between screw hooks. Insert dowel into curtain rod pocket. Mount curtain on screw hooks.

8

Cut two box ends 4½" (11.5 cm) long from 1 × 4 pine. Cut nine 20" (51 cm) slats from screen molding; sand all surfaces. Predrill nail holes ⅜" (1 cm) from each end of each slat, using ¹⁄₁₆" drill bit.

9

Secure three slats to one long side of box end, using a small amount of wood glue and brads; center one slat, and align others to outer edges. Repeat for two short sides. Attach opposite ends of slats to other box end.

10

Paint window box as desired; allow to dry. Paint and apply dimensional bugs and flowers, if desired. Secure sawtooth hangers to the back end edges of the top slat. Apply bumpers to lower slats so box will hang level. Hang window box under mirror; place pails in window box.

MATERIALS

- Two twin flat sheets of different pastel colors
- Paper for drawing patterns
- ¹⁄₄ yd. (0.25 m) paper-backed fusible web
- 1 yd. (0.92 m) fabric, 45" (115 cm) wide, for cover ties
- ¹⁄₄ yd. (0.25 m) each of five to eight fabrics, 45" (115 cm) wide, for appliqués
- ¹⁄₄ yd. (0.25 m) fabric, 45" (115 cm) wide, for ties on each pillowcase
- 36" × 45" (91.5 × 115 cm) extra-loft batting
- Temporary spray adhesive for fabric
- Tear-away stabilizer
- 2 yd. (1.85 m) narrow twill tape and four small plastic rings, for securing comforter inside cover
- Thread

TOOLS

- Scissors
- Sewing machine
- Iron
- Safety pins

Flower Appliqué Comforter Cover

This one-of-a-kind bedding ensemble features a comforter cover accented with cheerful raised flower and butterfly appliqués and generous fabric ties. Designer touches like this are usually costly, but you can make it economically because the front and back of the cover are made from two twin-size flat sheets. Generally the sheets are slightly narrower and slightly longer than a standard comforter, so with some simple adjustments, the comforter will fit snugly inside the new cover. Pillowcases are embellished with coordinating bows.

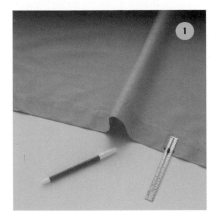

HOW TO MAKE A FLOWER APPLIQUÉ COMFORTER COVER

1

Prewash sheets and pillowcases. Check to see that the pastel sheets are the same width; trim one sheet, if necessary. On the sheet that will become the top front of the cover, mark positions for buttonholes in the center of the top hem, 4" (10 cm) in from each side. Divide the space between the marks into four equal spaces; mark. Stitch buttonholes, 1¼" (3.2 cm) long, at marks, perpendicular to the edge.

2

On the wrong side of the sheet, mark a line 25" (63.5 cm) from the upper edge; this will become the upper fold of the cover. Mark a line 63½" (161.3 cm) below the first line; trim off excess. On the other sheet, mark a line 63" (160 cm) below the top hem; this will become the lower fold of the cover. Mark a line 25½" (64.8 cm) below the first line; trim off excess.

3

Enlarge the patterns for the flower and butterfly on paper; cut out. Cut a 2½" (6.5 cm) strip from the end of each appliqué fabric. Fuse paper-backed fusible web to the wrong side of each strip. Trace four butterfly bodies and nine flower centers on the paper backing; cut out.

(Continued)

BUTTERFLY: Body, Wings

FLOWER: Center, Petals

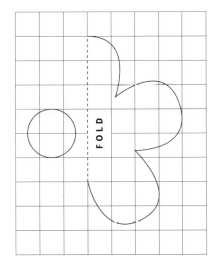

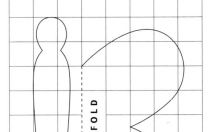

APPLIQUÉ PATTERNS: 1 Square=1" (2.5 cm)

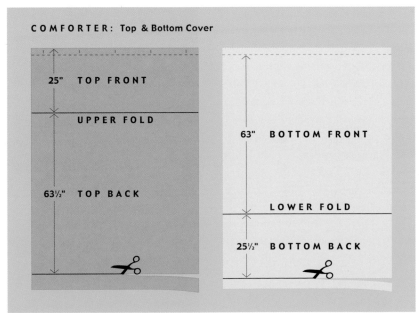

COMFORTER: Top & Bottom Cover

25" TOP FRONT

UPPER FOLD

63½" TOP BACK

63" BOTTOM FRONT

LOWER FOLD

25½" BOTTOM BACK

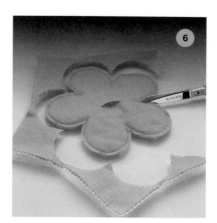

HOW TO MAKE A FLOWER APPLIQUÉ COMFORTER COVER
(Continued)

4

Cut twenty-six 9" (23 cm) squares of assorted fabrics for the dimensional appliqués. Cut thirteen 9" (23 cm) squares of batting. Trace nine flowers and four butterflies on the wrong side of half of the fabric squares.

5

Apply a light coat of temporary spray adhesive to the wrong side of the unmarked squares and adhere the batting. Cut a 1½" (3.8 cm) slit in the center of the marked squares. Pin the marked squares to the batted squares, right sides together; mix colors randomly. With batting facing down, stitch on marked line, using a short stitch.

6

Trim away excess fabric to within ¼" (6 mm) of stitching. Clip into corners up to but not through the stitches. Turn the shapes right side out through the slits. Press.

COMFORTER:
Appliqué Arrangement

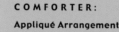

7

Remove the paper backing from the fusible web on the flower centers and butterfly bodies. Fuse the pieces in place on the sides opposite the slits.

8

Position the flowers and butterflies on the bottom front sheet of the cover, arranging them randomly; use the diagram for a guide. Keep in mind that the center 39" (99 cm) of the sheet will actually be on the top of the bed. Pin in place, using safety pins.

9

Slip a piece of tear-away stabilizer under each appliqué. Secure the shapes to the sheet, stitching around the flower centers and butterfly bodies. Use a short, narrow zigzag, stitching over the outer edges or straight-stitch ⅛" (3 mm) from the edges.

10

Cut five 6½" × 36" (16.3 × 91.5 cm) strips of fabric on the lengthwise grain of the tie fabric. Fold a strip in half lengthwise, right sides together. Trim off ends at 45° angle. Stitch ¼" (6 mm) from the cut edges, leaving a 4" (10 cm) opening in the center. Repeat for each strip. Turn strips right side out through openings; stitch closed.

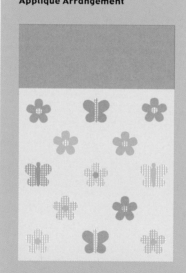

11

Overlap the hems of the sheets, right sides up, aligning edges to stitching lines; baste across the ends. Mark through the buttonholes for the positions of the ties. Make a pleat in the center of each tie, and stitch it in place securely, parallel to the hem.

12

Stitch the cut ends of the sheets, right sides together, in a ½" (1.3 cm) seam. Finish the seam allowances together and press in one direction.

13

Fold the sheets, right sides together, on the marked lines; pin the sides together. (The seam will shift to the back.) Stitch narrow seams, just inside the selvages. If one selvage has been trimmed, finish those seam allowances together. Turn the cover right side out.

14

Press the upper and lower folds. Cut four 18" (46 cm) pieces of twill tape. Fold each strip in half and pin them inside the cover in each corner. Stitch ¼" (6 mm) from the upper and lower folds, catching the twill tape in the stitching.

15

Securely stitch a plastic ring to each corner of the comforter. Insert the comforter into the cover; tie the twill tape to the rings. Pull the tie ends through the buttonholes, and tie bows.

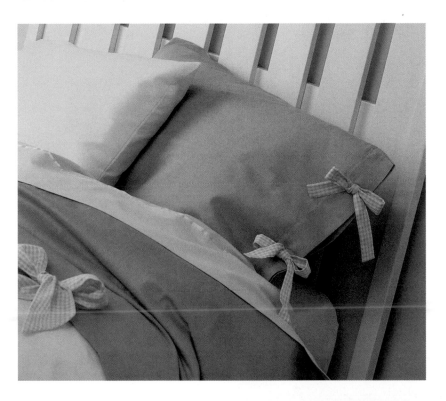

HOW TO EMBELLISH PILLOWCASES

1

Cut three 2½" (6.5 cm) strips on the crosswise grain for pillow ties; cut each strip in half. Fold a strip in half lengthwise, right sides together. Stitch ¼" (6 mm) from the cut edges, leaving a 2" (5 cm) opening in the center. Repeat for each strip. Turn strips right side out through openings; stitch closed.

2

Mark positions for three buttonholes in the center of the front pillowcase hem; place outer marks 3" (7.5 cm) from the ends and one in the center. Stitch ½" (1.3 cm) buttonholes perpendicular to the hem edge.

3

Mark through the buttonholes for the positions of the ties on the wrong side of the back hem. Make a pleat in the center of each tie and stitch it in place, parallel to the hem.

4

Insert the pillow. Pull tie ends through buttonholes, and tie bows.

Window Treatment

Resembling little canopies, simple rod-pocket valances are mounted on curved rods at the window tops. For the best effect, plan the valance length to be about one-fifth of the distance from the top of the window treatment to the floor. White bifold shutters offer privacy and light control for the lower half of the window. Home centers usually carry a range of sizes that can be adjusted to fit, with complete information for installing them.

MATERIALS

- Washable fabric to coordinate with the bedding; amount determined in steps 1 and 2, opposite
- Thread
- Curved curtain rod and mounting brackets

TOOLS

- Scissors
- Carpenter's square
- Sewing machine
- Iron
- Drill and drill bits; screwdriver

HOW TO MAKE A ROD-POCKET CANOPY VALANCE

1

Mount the curtain rod on the wall just outside the window frame. Measure the curved surface of the rod. Multiply this measurement by 2½; divide by the fabric width, and round up or down to the nearest whole number, to determine the number of fabric widths necessary.

2

Determine the desired finished length of the valance, usually 15" to 17" (38 to 43 cm) long; add 7½" (19.3 cm) to determine the cut lengths of the pieces. Multiply the number of widths needed by the cut length to determine the amount of fabric needed for one canopy.

3

Prewash the fabric. Measure and cut the lengths, using a carpenter's square to ensure straight edges. Trim away the selvages. Seam together the number of fabric widths needed, using ½" (1.3 cm) seams; finish the seam allowances together and press to one side.

4

Press under the lower edge 4" (10 cm). Unfold the pressed edge and turn the cut edge back, aligning it to the pressed foldline; press the outer fold. Refold the hem, encasing the raw edge to form a 2" (5 cm) double-fold hem.

5

Stitch along the inner fold. Press and stitch 1" (2.5 cm) double-fold side hems.

FLOWER BOOKENDS

Made like the beetle bookends on page 64, these bookends have a flower split between them. Use the flower pattern on page 25.

6

Turn under the upper edge ½" (1.3 cm). Then turn under again 3" (7.5 cm); pin. Stitch along the inner fold. Stitch again 1½" (3.8 cm) from the outer fold, forming the rod pocket and heading.

7

Insert the curved rod into the rod pocket. Mount the rod on the brackets. Adjust the canopy fullness evenly.

MATERIALS

- Two sheets 12" × 18" (30.5 × 46 cm) craft foam, 2 mm thick; one yellow and one orange

- One sheet of yellow 8" × 12" (20.5 × 30.5 cm) craft foam, 3 mm thick

- Clock movement for a $1/4$" (6 mm) thick clock face; battery

- Decorative clock hands, optional

- Foam numbers, 1" (2.5 cm) tall or paint pens

- Craft glue

TOOLS

- Scissors or craft knife and cutting board

- Awl, optional

Sun Clock

The sun is always shining in this delightful garden bedroom. This friendly fellow also tells the time.

HOW TO MAKE A SUN CLOCK

1

Enlarge and cut out the pattern. From the 2 mm foam, cut out a yellow sun and an orange sun. From the 3 mm foam, cut out a 6" (15 cm) circle.

2

Layer the orange sun over the yellow sun, staggering the points to create a sun with twelve equally spaced points. Secure layers together, using craft glue.

3

Adhere the circle to the center of the sun. Adhere numbers one through twelve on the sun points or write the numbers, using paint pens.

4

Punch a hole in the exact center of the sun, using an awl, or cut an X, using a craft knife. Insert the stem of the clock movement through the hole from the sun back. Adhere the movement to the clock back, making sure that the clock will hang with the 12 at the top. Secure the stem washer to the clock front, compressing the foam as necessary.

5

Attach the clock hands, following the manufacturer's directions. Install the battery and set the proper time. Hang the clock.

SUN: Rays

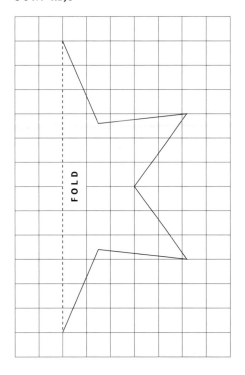

FOLD

CLOCK PATTERN: 1 Square=1" (2.5 cm)

SWITCH PLATE

A wooden birdhouse switch plate, found at a craft store, is decked out with painted wooden shapes to give it charm and dimension.

Birdhouse Shelves

Quaint birdhouses perch at the ends
of a shelf while providing
support for the shelf above. Backed
by a picket fence section, the
double-shelf unit provides a place
for showcasing a favorite collection.

MATERIALS

- Two birdhouses; not necessary
  to be identical, but must be the
  same height
- Two 36" (91.5 cm) pine shelves
- Two wooden shelf brackets
- 36" (91.5 cm) length of short
  picket fencing
- Wood screws
- Primer; latex semigloss base
  coat paint; craft paints
- Sawtooth hangers; nails
  or screws
- Molly bolts or anchors for
  securing shelf to wall

TOOLS

- Sandpaper
- Paintbrushes
- Drill; drill bits
- Saw
- Screwdriver

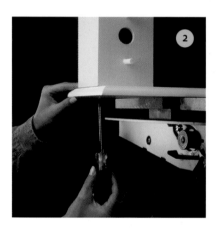

HOW TO MAKE A
BIRDHOUSE SHELF

1
Cut pointed stakes from lower edge of
picket fence even with bottom of other
pickets. Sand and prime all wood surfaces.
Paint the shelves, brackets, birdhouses,
and picket fence with a base coat of paint.

2
Secure birdhouses to center ends of
one shelf, using flathead wood screws.
Predrill holes through the shelf, and
insert screws from the shelf bottom.

3
Center fence behind shelf, aligning lower
edges. Secure fence to shelf, using screws;
predrill holes through end and center
pickets into center of back shelf edge.

4
Place second shelf on top of birdhouses.
Secure fence to second shelf, using screws;
predrill holes through outer and middle
pickets into center of back shelf edge.

5
Secure sawtooth hangers to back of fence.
Mount shelf brackets on wall, 32"
(81.5 cm) apart at wall studs, or use molly
bolts or anchors for support. Center shelf
unit on brackets; mark location of sawtooth
hangers. Remove shelves; insert screws
or nails for hangers. Replace shelf unit.

Birdhouse Grow Chart

Anchored to the wall, a pole topped with a cute birdhouse provides a place to keep track of a little girl's growth.

MATERIALS

- Wooden craft birdhouse
- 1 × 2 pine board, 60" (152.5 cm) long
- Primer; base coat paint; craft paints
- 60" (152.5 cm) tape measure
- 2½" (6.5 cm) drywall screws
- Glue
- Sawtooth hanger for mounting birdhouse

TOOLS

- Paintbrushes
- Drill and drill bits
- Carpenter's level
- Screwdriver; hammer

HOW TO MAKE A BIRDHOUSE GROW CHART

1

Sand, prime, and paint the birdhouse and pine post as desired. Position the post on the wall, just above and perpendicular to the base board; use a carpenter's level for accuracy. To avoid having to use wall anchors, position the post over a wall stud. Secure by inserting three or four drywall screws off-center, where they will be covered by the tape measure.

2

Attach a sawtooth hanger to the back of the birdhouse. Mount the birdhouse to the wall above the post, with the house bottom resting on the post top.

3

Determine the distance from the post bottom to the floor. Cut this amount from the end of the tape measure. Glue the tape measure to one side of the post, aligning the cut end of the tape measure to the post bottom.

To give her room a
personal touch,
wooden letters and
shapes are painted
and glued to a
wooden plaque.

MATERIALS

- Eight 1 × 4 pine boards, 48"
  (122 cm) long
- Two 2 × 4 boards, 40"
  (102 cm) long
- Two 2 × 4 boards, 12"
  (30.5 cm) long
- Two 2 × 2 posts, 60"
  (152.5 cm) long
- Two ball knob finials
- Primer; white paint
- Screws
- Two connecting screws
- Four carriage bolts with nuts
  and washers

TOOLS

- Saw
- Sandpaper
- Paintbrush
- Drill and drill bits

Picket Fence Headboard

Standing guard over the "flower bed" is a sturdy picket fence
headboard. Pine boards are shaped into dog-ear pickets,
and secured to sturdy crosswise supports. Ball knobs perched
atop high posts flank each side of the fence.

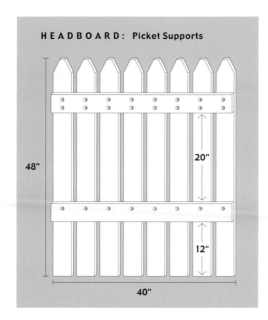

HEADBOARD: Picket Supports

48"

20"

12"

40"

HEADBOARD: Attachment Supports

HOW TO MAKE A PICKET FENCE HEADBOARD

1

Cut the corners from the tops of the pine boards to make dog-ear pickets. Sand the boards. Prime all wood surfaces; allow to dry. Paint the boards white; allow to dry.

2

Arrange the pickets parallel to each other and evenly spaced on the work surface, with the outer edges of the outer pickets 40" (102 cm) apart. Place the 40" (102 cm) 2×4 supports over the pickets, 20" (51 cm) apart and perpendicular to the pickets, with the lower support 12" (30.5 cm) above the bottom of the pickets. Secure the upper support to the pickets, inserting two screws through the support into each picket. Secure one screw through the lower support into each picket.

3

Turn the headboard over. Insert another screw through each picket into the lower support.

4

Position the headboard next to the bed frame; mark for the location of the bolt holes. Place the headboard face-up on the work surface; position the short 2×4 supports under the support at the bottom of the outer pickets. Secure the pickets to the short supports, inserting three screws through each picket into the support; avoid the area near the hole marks.

5

Secure the ball knobs to the post tops, using connecting screws. Place the posts alongside the headboard, aligning the bottoms. Predrill holes through the posts into the center of the support ends; secure with long screws.

6

Drill holes through the pickets and short supports for the carriage bolts, using a bit slightly larger than the bolt. Attach the headboard to the bed frame.

Watering Can Lamp

Lamps can be fashioned from a wide variety of items, including some rather unlikely candidates. This whimsical watering can, for example, easily becomes a one-of-a-kind bedside lamp. For best results, use a watering can that has a flat or slightly rounded partial cover through which the lamp pipe can be supported. Individual parts or kits for making lamps are available at specialty lamp stores, home improvement stores, and some craft stores.

Fabric flowers are adhered to the outer surface of the lamp shade, coordinating it with other items in the room.

MATERIALS

- Galvanized watering can
- Lamp pipe, 3" to 6" (7.5 cm to 15 cm) long
- Two washers to fit lamp pipe
- Neck, 2" (5 cm) long
- Socket cap
- Socket with insulating sleeve
- Electrical lamp cord with wall plug
- Adhesive base pad
- Clip-on lamp shade
- Fabric scraps in various pastel colors
- Spray adhesive

TOOLS

- Drill; ½" and ¼" drill bits
- Screwdriver
- Wire stripper

HOW TO MAKE A WATERING CAN LAMP

1

Mark the placement for the pipe hole in the center of the watering can top. Drill a hole, using the ½" drill bit.

2

Mark the placement at the back of the can, ½" (1.3 cm) from the bottom, for the electrical cord. Drill a hole, using the ¼" drill bit.

3

Screw the socket cap to one end of the pipe; tighten the set screw. Add the neck, and secure a washer to the pipe below them. Thread the electrical cord through the back hole, through the other washer, through the top hole, and then through the lamp pipe.

4

Insert the lamp pipe through top hole. Thread lower washer onto lamp pipe; tighten until pipe is held firmly in place.

5

Split the cord end along the middle of the insulation; separate the halves for 2" (5 cm). Remove ½" to ¾" (1.3 to 2 cm) of insulation from the ends, using a wire stripper.

6

Tie an underwriter's knot by forming an overhand loop with one cord and an underhand loop with the other cord; insert each cord end through the loop of the other.

7

Loosen the terminal screws on the socket. Loop the wire on the ribbed side of the cord around the silver screw; tighten the screw. Loop the wire on the rounded side of the cord around the gold screw; tighten the screw. Make sure all strands of wire are wrapped around screws.

8

Adjust the underwriter's knot snug against the base of the socket; position the socket in the socket cap. Slide the insulating sleeve and outer shell over the socket with the terminal screws fully covered and the sleeve slot aligned over the switch. Press the socket assembly down into the socket cap until it locks into place.

9

Cut a piece of self-adhesive felt to fit the lamp bottom; secure.

10

Cut several fabric flowers or butterflies, using the patterns on page 25; reduce the size as needed. Spray the wrong side with permanent adhesive. Apply to the outer surface of the lamp shade as desired. Insert the light bulb into the lamp. Attach the clip-on lamp shade.

YOUNG KIDS THINK SCHOOL'S
pretty cool, and playing teacher is a favorite
pastime. How awesome to have a bedroom with
all the trappings of an honest-to-goodness
classroom, where readin', 'ritin', and 'rithmetic
are all in a day's play! A budding artist can create
to her heart's content and a serious thinker
can ponder the universe amid his collection of
books and maps. A handy chalkboard wall is
an open slate for make-believe and an alphabet
wall border adds authentic schoolhouse flavor.

ABCs & 123s

Make bright fake fur rugs in geometric shapes, following the directions on page 106.

Make bright fake fur rugs in geometric shapes, following the directions on page 106.

MATERIALS

- Two twin flat sheets
- Twin sized extra-loft quilt batting
- 49 buttons (sew-through style), ³/₄" (2 cm) or larger diameter, in colors to match headboard crayons
- Temporary spray adhesive for fabric
- Masking tape

TOOLS

- Safety pins
- Straight pins
- Sewing machine with walking foot and button foot
- Removable marker
- Scissors
- Point turner

Button-quilted Coverlet

Even if you've never quilted before, this coverlet is easy to make. Batting is secured between two flat sheets with rows of channel quilting around the lower edges. An array of buttons dots the bed-top surface, echoing the colors of the headboard crayons.

RICKRACK PILLOWCASES & BED SKIRT

Apply jumbo black rickrack over the pillowcase hems and about 1" (2.5 cm) up from the bottom of a purchased bed skirt. Pin or glue-baste the trim in place, and stitch down the center. Prevent cut ends from raveling with liquid fray preventer, and turn them under, abutting ends that meet.

CRAYON HEADBOARD

Make this colorful headboard, following the directions for the picket fence headboard on page 34, omitting the outer posts. Cut the board tops to a slightly sharper point to resemble crayons, and paint them each a different color.

HOW TO MAKE A BUTTON-QUILTED COVERLET

1
Prewash the sheets. Cut to 70" × 91" (178 × 231.5 cm), or as wide as the wider sheet. Remove the selvages. If necessary for length, remove stitching from the upper hem. Curve the lower corners using a dinner plate as a guide.

2
Mark a line on the right side of the top sheet 6½" (16.3 cm) from the outer edges. Use the dinner plate to round the lower corners. Mark another line 6" (15 cm) from the first line. Following the diagram, mark dots for the button locations.

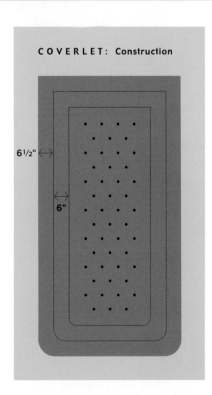

COVERLET: Construction

6½"

6"

3
Lightly steam the batting, if necessary. Spread out on a large flat surface; spray with temporary spray adhesive. Smooth the top sheet, right side up, over the batting.

4
Place the backing sheet over the top sheet, right sides together, aligning edges; pin. Trim away excess batting.

(Continued)

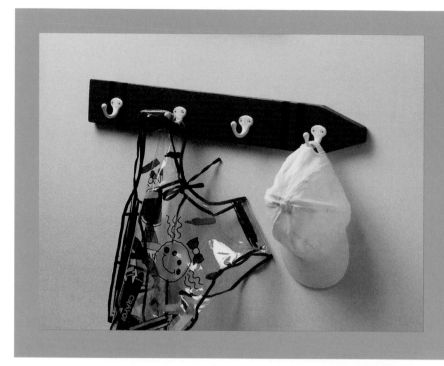

CRAYON WALL HOOKS

This unique wall hook board looks like a crayon or a pencil, depending on how you paint it. Shape the point like the headboard crayons, paint it the desired color, and attach hooks. Secure the hook crayon to the wall with screws at wall studs or with molly bolts.

HOW TO MAKE A BUTTON-QUILTED COVERLET (Continued)

5

Stitch ½" (1.3 cm) seam around the outer edge, stitching with the batting side down. Leave a 15" (38 cm) opening on one side for turning. Trim batting up to the seamline in the opening; trim batting along seams to ⅛" (3 mm). Trim corners diagonally.

6

Turn the backing seam allowance back and press lightly. Press under both edges of the opening ½" (1.3 cm).

7

Turn coverlet right side out through the opening. Gently push corners out, using a point turner. Push seams to edge and press edges lightly. Pin opening closed; edgestitch or slipstitch.

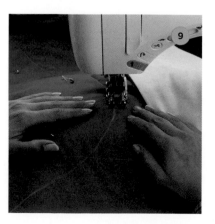

8

Place quilt right side up on flat surface. Starting at the center, pin layers together with safety pins every 4" to 8" (10 to 20.5 cm); avoid pinning too near marked lines and dots.

9

Set the sewing machine for 2.5 mm stitch length; reduce presser foot pressure slightly. Using a walking foot, stitch on the outer marked line. Repeat for the inner marked line.

10

Return the coverlet to the flat surface and arrange the buttons. Secure each to the coverlet, using masking tape. Roll the coverlet from one side to the center, so it will fit under the arm of your sewing machine.

11

Set the sewing machine for sewing on buttons. Beginning in the center, stitch the buttons to the coverlet, removing the tape for each button as you come to it.

APPLE LAMP SHADE & SWITCH PLATE

Use leftover project paints to customize accessories like this lamp shade and chalkboard switch plate. Then dress them up with painted wooden apples. After lettering the switch plate with chalk, spray it with an aerosol sealer.

Arithmetic Window Cornices

Fabric-covered wooden cornices top these windows, hiding the hardware for fabric roller shades. The shades are made and mounted as on page 70 before mounting the cornice. Painted wooden shapes secured to the cornice fronts playfully illustrate simple arithmetic problems. The entire window treatment is made without taking a single stitch. All you need are some basic carpentry and crafting skills.

MATERIALS

- ½" (1.3 cm) plywood
- Outside corner molding
- Wood glue; 16 × 1½" (3.8 cm) brads
- Paint
- Fabric
- Lightweight batting
- Spray adhesive
- Wooden shapes, such as apples or stars; craft sticks, for arithmetic problems
- Two 4" (10 cm) angle irons

TOOLS

- Miter box and back saw
- Hammer
- Drill and bits
- Staple gun and staples

CORNICE: Construction

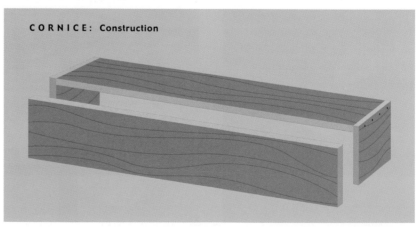

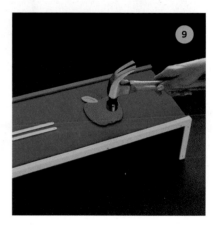

HOW TO MAKE AN ARITHMETIC CORNICE

1
Cut plywood for the cornice top 5" (12.7 cm) long and 2" (5 cm) wider than the window frame width. Cut two 5" × 9" (12.7 × 23 cm) end pieces; cut a front piece 9" (23 cm) long and 1" (2.5 cm) wider than the top. Glue each side piece to the top piece, aligning upper edges; secure with nails. Glue front to top and sides; secure with nails.

2
Place a piece of corner molding on upper edge of cornice; mark a line on the cornice front and sides at edge of molding. Repeat on the lower edge.

3
Cut a batting strip to fit between the lines the same length as the distance across the top and sides. Affix the batting to the cornice, using spray adhesive.

4
Cut a 9" (23 cm) wide strip of fabric 8" (20.5 cm) longer than the distance across the front and sides of the cornice. Center fabric on cornice; secure with staples at center front, close to top and bottom. Smooth fabric taut to one end; secure with staples near top and bottom of cornice end. Repeat for opposite side.

5
Wrap fabric around the ends to the inside of the cornice, mitering corner at upper edge; glue in place. Repeat for opposite side. Allow glue to dry; remove staples.

6
Glue the raw edge of the fabric to the top of the cornice; allow to dry. Smooth fabric taut to the lower edge; glue in place.

7
Cut a fabric strip with the width equal to the inside height of the cornice plus ½" (1.3 cm), long enough to fit the inside of the front and sides of the cornice. Secure, using spray adhesive.

8
Cut molding strips to fit the top and bottom edges of the cornice, mitering the corners. Paint moldings as desired. Secure moldings to cornice, using finishing nails; predrill holes with ⅟₁₆" drill bit. Apply wood glue to mitered edges.

9
Cut craft sticks to make arithmetic symbols. Paint wooden shapes and symbols for arithmetic problems. Secure to cornice front, using finishing nails; predrill holes.

10
Mount angle irons on wall, at the top and just outside the window frame. Position cornice over angle irons; mark location of screw holes on cornice. Remove cornice from wall; predrill holes. Reposition cornice, and insert screws through angle irons into cornice.

Chalkboard Wall

In the little artist's corner, chalkboard paint turns the wall into an oversized space for drawing and playing school. Painted directly onto the wall, the chalkboard is outlined with a border of half-round molding that echoes the alphabet border higher on the wall.

MATERIALS

- Chalkboard spray paint
- Semigloss latex paint
- Painter's masking tape; newspaper
- Half-round molding

TOOLS

- Paintbrushes
- Carpenter's level
- Miter box and back saw

HOW TO MAKE A BORDERED CHALKBOARD

1
Mark a large rectangle on the wall for the chalkboard, taking into consideration the height of the child's reach; use a level for accuracy. Mask off rectangle; tape newspaper to surrounding area to protect the wall from overspray.

2
Paint the rectangle with chalkboard paint, following the manufacturer's directions. Allow to dry and cure.

3
Cut half-round molding strips to fit the outer edge of the chalkboard, mitering the corners. Paint the strips one of the colors used in the wall border. Secure to the wall as in step 3, opposite.

Alphabet Wall Border

The walls of this bedroom are an interactive learning and play area, so they are painted with kid-friendly semi-gloss paints that are easy to keep clean. Half-round molding painted with bright primary colors accents the alphabet border near the top of the wall. We planned our border to line up with the window cornices, creating a continuous line.

HOW TO PAINT AN ALPHABET WALL BORDER

1

Paint the walls with a base coat of semigloss paint; allow to dry. Using a level, mark a line around the room, even with the cornice or window frame top. Mark another line even with the cornice bottom or 9" (23 cm) below the first one; mark a third line 1½" (3.8 cm) below the second one.

2

Cut half-round molding to fit the three marked lines, mitering at the corners. Paint the molding strips red, yellow, and blue, repeating the colors of the cornice. Allow to dry.

3

Predrill holes in molding every 16" (40.5 cm) where they will align to wall studs, using ¹⁄₁₆" bit. Nail molding strips to wall, using finishing nails. Countersink nails, using a nail set. Touch up nail holes and mitered corners with paint.

4

Cut self-adhesive letters apart; do not remove backing. Beginning at the middle of one wall with the letter M, position the letters temporarily, using masking tape. When you are satisfied with the placement, remove protective backing and adhere letters. Follow the manufacturer's tips for letter placement. Repeat on another wall with numbers, if desired.

Self-dispensing Paper Roller

Wide paper for drawing or coloring is always available, thanks to this handy self-dispensing roller mounted on the wall. The paper is kept close to the wall behind a dowel at the base of the brackets, and a strip of screen molding lower on the wall provides an edge for tearing off finished artwork.

MATERIALS

- Paper roll on a cardboard tube, 24" (61 cm) wide
- Wooden pole wall brackets; molly bolts or toggle anchors for hanging, if not mounted at wall studs
- 1" (2.5 cm) dowel, 26" (66 cm) long
- Finials or balls to fit 1" (2.5 cm) dowel
- ½" (1.3 cm) wooden dowel, 25" (63.5 cm) long
- Wood glue
- Screen molding, 26" (66 cm) long; molly bolts or toggle anchors for hanging, if not mounted at wall studs
- Two plastic washers for spacers

TOOLS

- Drill and bits
- Screwdriver

HOW TO MAKE A SELF-DISPENSING PAPER ROLLER

1

Paint the brackets, dowels, finials, and screen molding as desired; allow to dry. Drill a hole near the lower, back, inside edge of the pole bracket to ⅜" (1 cm) depth, using ½" drill bit; wrap masking tape around the bit to mark the depth. Repeat in the same place on the inside edge of the other bracket.

2

Apply a small amount of wood glue in the bracket holes. Insert the ½" (1.3 cm) dowel ends into the holes.

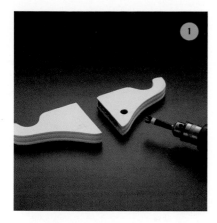

3

Mount the brackets on the wall at the desired height, screwing into wall studs. Or use molly bolts or toggle anchors if not installing into wall studs.

4

Mount the screen molding directly below the brackets, the desired distance from the floor; predrill holes ½" (1.3 cm) from the ends, and place washers between the molding and the wall to act as spacers.

5

Predrill holes in ends of 1" (2.5 cm) dowel; attach finials. Insert dowel through paper roll tube; mount on brackets. Feed paper behind lower dowel and under screen molding.

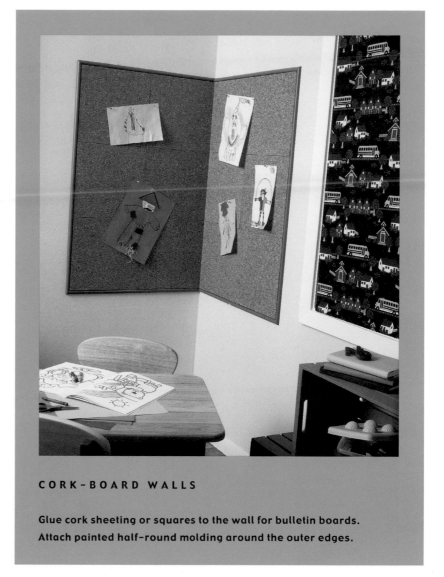

CORK-BOARD WALLS

Glue cork sheeting or squares to the wall for bulletin boards. Attach painted half-round molding around the outer edges.

Canvas Grow Chart

This quick and easy fabric chart keeps track of your little one's growth with big, colorful numbers. There is also plenty of space for recording life's special moments or listing favorite books and games. Sewing isn't necessary when you use outdoor canvas that is finished to a 32" (81.5 cm) width. Numbers and lines for the giant tape measure are stenciled on with opaque acrylic paints. Handy paint pens are used for marking your child's height and noting special events. When your child outgrows the chart, it can be rolled up and tucked away as a permanent keepsake.

MATERIALS

- 1 7/8 yd. (1.75 m) polyester outdoor canvas, 32" (81.5 cm) wide
- Fabric glue
- Three 3/8" (1 cm) grommets and grommet setting tool
- 4" (10 cm) number stencils
- Apple stencils
- Repositionable stencil adhesive spray
- Opaque acrylic paints or latex paints
- Three hooks

TOOLS

- Iron
- Straightedge
- Sponge pouncers or makeup sponges

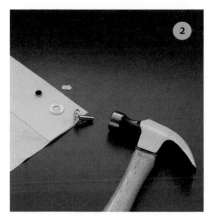

HOW TO MAKE A CANVAS GROW CHART

1
Fold under a 3" (7.5 cm) bottom hem on the canvas. Secure the hem with fabric glue. Repeat for the top hem.

2
Attach three grommets 1" (2.5 cm) below the top; center one grommet and position the others 3" (7.5 cm) from the edges.

3
Using a straightedge and a paint pen, mark off inches from the bottom hem up to five feet along the right side of the canvas. Make inch marks 2" (5 cm) long; make foot marks 4" (10 cm) long.

4
Stencil numbers alongside the marks so that the tops of the numbers are even with the foot marks. Stencil apples along the left side of the chart.

5
Hold the grow chart up to the wall so the bottom hem touches the floor. Mark for the location of the hooks. Secure hooks to the wall; mount the chart.

A TO Z BOOKENDS

Painted wooden letters A and Z are used to create bookends as on page 64. Purchase large letters at a craft store. Sand them smooth before priming and painting.

Map Quilt

Every classroom needs a map. This one is a fabric panel manufactured by Fabric Traditions, available at fabric and craft stores. We have quilted it for extra dimension and sewn in ribbons for hanging.

HOW TO MAKE A MAP QUILT

1

Press map panel and backing. Square the map panel and cut backing fabric to the same size. Lightly steam the batting, if necessary. Spread batting out on a flat surface; spray with temporary adhesive. Smooth the map panel, right side up, over the batting.

2

Cut six 8" (20.5 cm) pieces of ribbon. Fold ribbons in half and pin them, evenly spaced, to the panel top, with the end pieces ¾" (2 cm) from the sides. Pin the backing over the map panel, right sides together. Trim away excess batting, if necessary.

3

Stitch ¼" (6 mm) seam around the outer edge, stitching with the backing side up. Leave 10" (25.5 cm) opening on one side for turning. Trim batting up to seamline in opening. Trim corners diagonally. Clip selvages, if necessary.

4

Turn the backing seam allowance back and press lightly. Press under both edges of opening ¼" (6 mm).

5

Turn map quilt right side out through the opening. Gently push corners out, using a point turner. Push seams to edge and press edges lightly. Pin opening closed; slipstitch.

6

Place quilt right side up on flat surface. Starting at the center, pin layers together with safety pins every 4" to 8" (10 to 20.5 cm).

7

Set the sewing machine for 2.5 mm stitch length; reduce presser foot pressure slightly. Thread the needle with monofilament thread; use regular thread in the bobbin. Using a walking foot, stitch around the U.S. border; stitch down the Mississippi River. Then stitch any other prominent lines between states, so there are quilting lines at least every 8" (20.5 cm).

8

Paint the wooden pole, finials, and brackets as desired. Mount the brackets on the wall. Insert the pole through the ribbon loops at the quilt top; hang the map quilt.

DRESSER DRAWER KNOBS

Paint wooden cubes in colors to match the headboard crayons, and secure them to the drawer fronts. As on page 69, use wooden spools as spacers behind the cubes.

MATERIALS

- Unpainted bench-style toy chest
- Wood primer
- School-bus yellow semigloss latex paint
- Gray, black, red, and white acrylic paints
- Silver spray paint
- Painter's masking tape
- Black, self-adhesive letters
- Two 7" (18 cm) wheels; bolts, washers, and acorn nuts to fit through axle hole
- Foam pipe insulation with adhesive strips
- Air return vent cover; screws
- Personalized license plate
- Two round reflectors; two rectangular reflectors
- Two round mirrors
- Small windshield wiper blades
- Masonite™
- Hinge

TOOLS

- Sandpaper; tack cloth
- Paintbrushes or foam applicators
- Sponge
- Hot glue gun
- Drill and drill bits
- Screwdriver

School Bus Toy Chest

A little imagination, paint, and a few unusual accessories have turned this wooden toy chest into a charming yellow school bus. Look for an unpainted bench-style toy chest with a solid back.

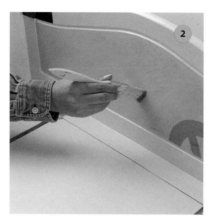

HOW TO MAKE A SCHOOL BUS TOY CHEST

1

Sand the entire toy chest inside and out. Vacuum off the surface; wipe with a tack cloth. Prime all surfaces. Mask off the "windshield" with painter's masking tape and newspaper. Paint all other surfaces yellow. Allow to dry.

2

Remove the mask from the windshield. Paint the windshield light gray; allow to dry. Paint the steering wheel a darker gray. Using a dry brush and the darker gray paint, lightly stroke in different directions to make window reflections.

3

Mask off ½" (1.3 cm) stripes to outline the hood and side door on the bus. Sponge on black paint between the tapes.

4

Position wheels on each side of the chest, near the front, so the wheels rest on the floor. Mark through the wheel centers. Drill holes at the marks. Secure wheels to the chest, using bolts, washers, and acorn nuts.

5

Spray-paint an air return vent cover with silver paint for a grill. Secure the grill to the center front of the chest, using wood screws. Secure a personalized license plate below the grill.

8

Remove the rubber strip from the windshield wipers. Hot-glue the wipers at angles to the windshield. Adhere letters spelling "school bus" above the windshield.

9

Make a small stop sign following the directions on page 66. Secure the sign to the side of the bus with a hinge.

6

Attach two round adhesive-backed mirrors on each side of the grill for headlights; apply smaller rectangular reflectors below the headlights for signal lights. Attach round reflectors above the upper corners of the windshield.

7

Cut pipe insulation to fit the bottom front of the chest. Remove paper backing from adhesive on one side of slit; secure to chest front. Repeat for other side of slit.

STORAGE CRATES

Create plenty of storage room for books, art materials, and games with wooden storage crates. Purchase plain crates from a craft store; sand, prime, and paint them in bright colors to match the headboard crayons. Then stack them as desired. Purchase plastic or metal buckets for holding crayons, markers, and chalk. These can easily be toted to the table, paper dispenser, or chalkboard as needed.

Bedrooms

for COOL KIDS

LITTLE BOYS ARE FASCINATED

with the world of wheels; cars and trucks of all

sorts and sizes fuel their fantasies and drive their

dreams. With a paintbrush and a few minor

construction projects, you can create the perfect

haven for your little motorhead. Decorated in

classic DMV motif, his personal stretch of highway

is zoned for all the activities a little guy gets into.

Not just another nighttime pit stop, his bedroom

is a personal refuge where he can idle away

quiet hours or rev his motor with a crew of buddies.

Motorhead Haven

Walls & Woodwork

Two subtle shades of gray painted on the walls are divided by chair rail molding that has been painted with black and yellow road construction stripes. In the play area, a roadway shelf, constructed from two rails of 1 × 4 lumber, provides a sturdy surface for driving and parking small cars and trucks. Along the roadway, dark gray shadows of cars and trucks are stenciled on the wall.

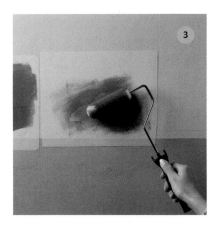

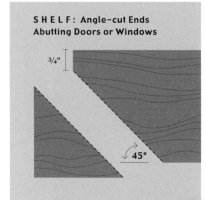

HOW MAKE THE ROADWAY SHELF WALL TREATMENT

1

Mark a line around the room 36" (91.5 cm) from the floor, using a carpenter's level for accuracy. Paint the wall above the line light gray. Paint the wall below the line medium gray. Allow to dry. Mark the line again, if necessary. In the area of the room where the roadway shelf will be placed, mark another line ¾" (2 cm) above the first.

2

Enlarge the die-cut figures so that trucks are about 10" (25.5 cm) long and cars are 6" to 7" (15 to 18 cm) long. From stencil blanks, cut a stencil of each design, simplifying them as necessary.

3

Spray the back of the stencil with repositionable stencil adhesive. Apply stencil to wall, with tires on the upper marked line. Paint stencil with dark gray paint, using foam roller. Repeat around the room, alternating stencils and varying the distance between them as desired.

4

Cut 1 × 4 lumber for chair rail molding to fit flat against wall around the room; angle-cut ends to join pieces and miter corners.

5

Cut 1 × 4 lumber to fit wall in area where roadway shelf will be placed; angle-cut ends to join pieces and miter corners. For ends that abut door or window moldings, mark ¾" (2 cm) from back edge; cut from mark to front edge at 45° angle (as above).

6

Sand all surfaces; wipe with tack cloth. Prime all surfaces; allow to dry. Paint the face and edges of the chair rail yellow; allow to dry. Beginning at one end of the chair rail, mark a 45° line. Place 2" (5 cm) masking tape along the line, wrapping onto the upper and lower edges. Continue masking off 2" (5 cm) stripes, leaving 2" (5 cm) stripes between for painting; keep a consistent 45° angle. Paint unmasked sections black. Remove masking tape; allow to dry thoroughly.

7

Sand and prime roadway shelf. Paint all surfaces black. Mask off a ⅜" (1 cm) stripe down the center of the shelf. Mask off 1" (2.5 cm) dashes, leaving 1" (2.5 cm) between them. Paint a white dashed line down the center of the shelf. Remove tape; allow to dry.

8

Place shelf over chair rail molding, aligning back edges. Secure together, using drywall screws.

9

Align chair rail to marked line on wall. Secure chair rail to wall, inserting drywall screws through wood into wall at stud locations. In area of shelf, top of shelf will align to upper marked line.

Wheel Clock

A unique wall clock is fashioned from a steering wheel cover and foam core board.

MATERIALS

- Steering wheel cover
- $\frac{1}{2}$" (1.3 cm) foam core board
- Silver tagboard
- Spray adhesive
- $\frac{1}{4}$" (6 mm) graphic tape
- $\frac{3}{4}$" (2 cm) number stickers
- Three large washers in graduated sizes with $\frac{5}{16}$" (7.5 mm) openings
- Clock movement for $\frac{3}{4}$" (2 cm) thick clock face; battery
- Decorative clock hands, optional
- Spray paint for coloring clock hands

TOOLS

- Mat knife and cutting surface
- Scissors
- Stylus or ballpoint pen
- Drill and bits
- Hot glue gun

HOW TO MAKE A WHEEL CLOCK

1

Remove the cardboard from the center of the steering wheel cover. Use it to trace a circle on the foam core board, tagboard, and tracing paper. Cut out the circles.

2

Adhere the tagboard circle to one side of the foam core circle. On the tracing paper circle, draw a circle 1½" (3.8 cm) from the outer edge and another circle 2½" (6.5 cm) from the outer edge. Mark twelve points, evenly spaced around the outer circle; draw spokes connecting points opposite each other.

3

Tape the tracing paper circle over the silver tagboard circle. Using a stylus or retracted ballpoint pen, trace the spokes from one side of the inner circle to the other, indenting the silver surface. Indent the points around the outer circle, indicating placement for the numbers.

4

Remove tracing paper. Adhere numbers with outer edges touching indented points. Cover the indented lines with graphic tape, stopping ½" (1.3 cm) from the center.

5

Drill a hole in the center of the clock face, large enough to accommodate the clock mechanism shaft. Insert the clock face into the steering wheel cover, working carefully around the circle.

6

Insert the stem of the clock movement through the hole from the back. Adhere the movement to the clock back. Place the three washers over the stem, layering from large to small. Secure the stem washer to the clock front.

WHEEL-BASE LAMP

The base of this ingenious lamp is a 7" (18 cm) steel wheel with a ½" (1.3 cm) diameter offset hub. Die-cut cars and trucks are glued to the black paper shade. Follow the general directions for assembling and wiring the lamp, as on page 36. Use a 12" (30.5 cm) lamp pipe and a socket that has a chain switch so you can hang a miniature wooden tire from the end. Using a drill bit suitable for metal, drill a hole through the recessed side of the hub and out through the tire for inserting the lamp cord.

7

Spray paint the clock hands, if desired; allow to dry. Attach the clock hands, following the manufacturer's directions. Install the battery and set the proper time. Hang the clock from the upper back of the steering wheel cover.

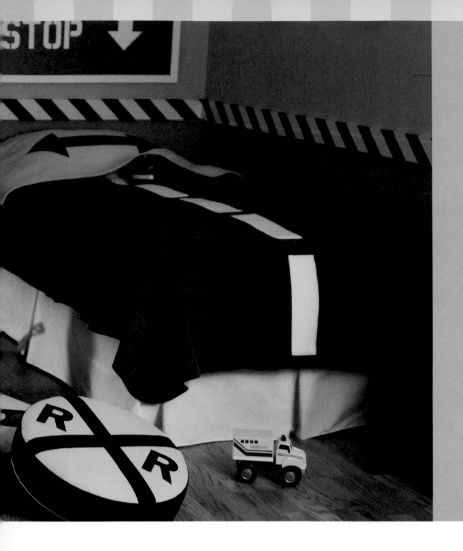

Roadway Coverlet

Cozy, cute, and easy to care for, this roadway coverlet is made by stitching together two layers of polyester fleece. Raw-edge appliqués are used to create the white line down the center of the gray road. The top of the extra-long coverlet is a reverse sham that simply folds down over the pillow, revealing the yellow underside, appliquéd with a double arrow traffic sign.

HOW TO SEW A ROADWAY COVERLET

1

Wash and dry all fabrics. Cut gray and yellow fabrics 116" (295 cm) long. Cut six strips of white fabric, 3½" × 12" (9 × 30.5 cm), with the long sides running on the lengthwise grain. Enlarge the double arrow pattern, opposite. Cut one double arrow from the black fleece.

2

Place the gray and yellow fabrics wrong sides together, aligning selvages and cut ends. Pin-baste the layers together about every 10" (25.5 cm), using safety pins. Trim off selvages evenly. Round the four corners, using a dinner plate as a guide.

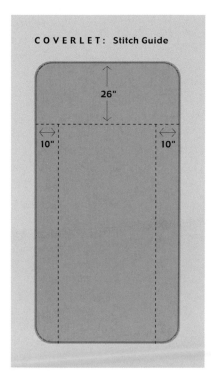

COVERLET: Stitch Guide

26"

10" 10"

ARROW

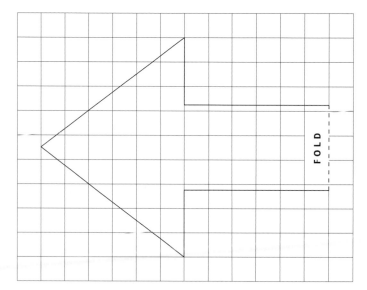

FOLD

3

Stitch ½" (1.3 cm) from the cut edges all around. Stitch again ¼" (6 mm) from the cut edges. Mark a line 26" (66 cm) from the top, using removable tape. Stitch on marked line. Mark lines running the lengthwise direction from the stitched line to the bottom, 10" (25.5 cm) from each side; stitch. Move or remove safety pins as you come to them.

4

Glue-baste the white strips up the center of the gray side, beginning 1½" (3.8 cm) from the bottom and ending 1½" (3.8 cm) from the horizontal stitching line, with 3" (7.5 cm) spaces between them. Stitch ⅛" (3 mm) from the edge around each white strip.

5

Glue-baste the arrow on the yellow side, in the center of the upper rectangle. Stitch ⅛" (3 mm) from the edge around the arrow. Remove the safety pins.

UNDER-BED STORAGE

Plastic under-bed storage boxes are jazzed up a little with reflector stickers. This box style has wheels and hinged lids for easy access.

Beetle Bookends

On a shelf or atop a desk or dresser, these husky bookends keep favorite books in order.

MATERIALS

- 1 × 6 pine board, 4' (1.23 m) long
- Tracing paper
- Primer for wood
- Acrylic or latex paints in desired colors
- Wood screws
- Self-adhesive vinyl bumpers
- Clear acrylic finish

TOOLS

- Jigsaw or coping saw
- Sandpaper; tack cloth
- Paintbrushes
- Drill and countersink bit
- Screwdriver

HOW TO MAKE BEETLE BOOKENDS

1
Cut 1 × 6 board into two 6½" (16.3 cm) bases and two 8½" (21.8 cm) uprights. Enlarge patterns; transfer to remaining board. Cut out car halves.

2
Sand all surfaces smooth; wipe with tack cloth. Prime all surfaces; allow to dry. Paint all surfaces; allow to dry.

3
Predrill three evenly spaced holes in uprights, ⅜" (1 cm) from lower edge, with outer holes ½" (1.3 cm) from sides; countersink holes. Butt base to upright; predrill holes in base edge. Attach base to upright.

BOOKEND
PATTERN:
1 Square=1"
(2.5 cm)

BEETLE BOOKENDS: Front & Back

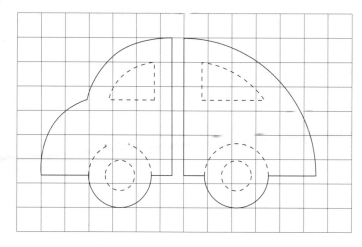

4

Predrill holes in upright centers 2" and 5" (5 and 12.7 cm) from tops, drilling from back; countersink holes. Place car halves in position in center of each bookend; predrill small holes into cars. Secure with screws.

5

Predrill holes in base centers, drilling from bottom up into wheels; counter-sink holes. Secure with screws.

6

Apply clear finish to all surfaces; allow to dry. Secure vinyl bumpers to bottom corners of bookends.

MIRROR

Reflectors add pizzazz to the mirror frame. See page 23 for mounting a mirror in a frame.

Traffic Signs

Traffic signs are easily made from 1/8" (3 mm) Masonite™. Paint signs for the quiet zone, play zone, work zone, or other activities. Use one of the signs shown here or look for inspiration as you drive.

HOW TO MAKE A TRAFFIC SIGN

1

Make a paper pattern for the sign; determine the size needed to accommodate the lettering or symbol. Cut Masonite into a square, rectangle, triangle, circle, or octagon, as desired. Sand edges smooth.

2

Prime the sign; allow to dry. Paint entire sign front with background color; allow to dry.

3

Enlarge pattern and trace symbol or letters on the sign. Paint symbol or letters by hand. Or, if letters will be stenciled, apply repositionable stencil adhesive to letter stencil backs, following the manufacturer's directions. Arrange stencils. Apply paint, using sponge applicator. Remove stencils; allow to dry.

4

Apply painter's masking tape the desired distance from the outer edge. Paint border, including cut edges. Allow to dry; remove tape.

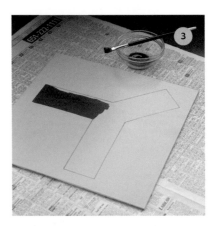

5

Apply clear finish, if desired; allow to dry. Predrill two holes at top and bottom. Mount sign, using screws; apply spacers to screws behind sign to make sign stand away from the wall.

TRAFFIC SIGNS: Playground, Y-intersection, Winding Road, & Stop

MATERIALS

- Masonite™ or ¼" (6 mm) plywood, cut 39" × 24" (99 × 61 cm)
- Primer
- Green or blue satin-finish or semigloss latex paint
- White acrylic craft paint
- 5" (12.7 cm) letter stencils
- Painter's masking tape
- Clear acrylic finish
- Molly bolts for hanging; ½" (1.3 cm) spacers

TOOLS

- Saw
- Sandpaper; tack cloth
- Drill and bits
- Paintbrushes

HOW TO MAKE A REST STOP HEADBOARD

1

Sand the wood; wipe with tack cloth. Prime all wood surfaces, allow to dry. Paint the headboard green or blue to resemble a highway sign.

2

Follow steps 3 to 5 for making and hanging signs on page 66. In step 3, mask off an arrow shape, using painter's masking tape. In step 5, predrill additional holes in the top and bottom center. Use molly bolts if screws will not be inserted into wall studs.

Rest Stop Headboard

A large highway sign points the way to a little boy's cozy resting spot. Similar to the other signs, this one doubles as a detached headboard.

Dresser Drawers with Tire Knobs

Transform an ordinary dresser by painting the drawer fronts in traffic-stopping red, yellow, and green. For a playful touch, replace the plain drawer pulls with these easy-to-make tire knobs.

MATERIALS

- Unpainted wooden wheels, 2" (5 cm) diameter, found in craft stores
- Unpainted wooden spools, ¾" (2 cm) high
- Craft paints in black and metallic silver
- Clear acrylic finish
- Dowel small enough to fit through wheels and spools; empty box
- Machine screws with lock washers and hex nuts for attaching to drawer fronts; length depends on drawer front thickness

TOOLS

- Artist's brushes

HOW TO MAKE TIRE DRAWER KNOBS

1
Paint the wooden wheels and spools black; allow to dry. For ease in painting and drying, insert a small dowel through the wheel and spool holes and suspend the dowel over a box.

2
Paint the centers of the wheels silver; allow to dry. Apply clear acrylic sealer to wheels and spools.

3
Insert machine screw through wheel and spool; secure to drawer front, using lock washer and hex nut. Repeat for each drawer.

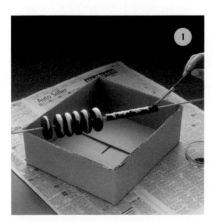

TIRE HOOKS

For a handy hanging place, secure tire knobs to a section of chair rail, using long wood screws.

Roller Shade & Display Shelf

This colorful, easy-to-operate window treatment is also as practical as they come. The roller shade controls the light and offers privacy while the board-mounted handkerchief valance provides a handy shelf for displaying vintage toy trucks, a collection of hubcaps, or other motorhead trophies.

The fabric roller shade is made from a kit that contains a fusible backing and a mounting roller with a pulley-system control for raising and lowering the shade. For an inside mounted shade, the window frame must be deep enough to accommodate the installed roller wrapped with the finished shade. If this is not the case, the shade can be installed as an outside mount, either to the front of the window frame or on the wall just beyond the frame.

HINT: Because the roller shade pulley cord is a continuous loop, it can pose a safety hazard to small children if not installed properly. Follow the manufacturer's directions and secure the loop to its tension clip flat against the window frame or wall.

HOW TO MAKE A ROLLER SHADE

1

Install the shade brackets, roller, pulley, and end plug at the window, following the manufacturer's directions. Measure the roller from the inside edge of the end plug to the inside edge of the pulley to determine the finished width of the shade. Steam-press the fabric thoroughly to preshrink it.

2

Using a carpenter's square to ensure perfectly squared corners, cut the fabric 2" (5 cm) wider than the desired finished width of the shade and 12" (30.5 cm) longer than the desired finished length. Cut the fusible backing 1" (2.5 cm) wider than the desired finished width of the shade and 12" (30.5 cm) longer than the desired finished length.

3

Fuse the backing to the wrong side of the fabric, centering it on the width of the fabric; fabric extends ½" (1.3 cm) beyond backing on each side. Use a press cloth, and follow the manufacturer's directions.

4

Mark the finished width of the shade on the backing. Cut on the marked lines. Apply liquid fray preventer to the edges sparingly, using a small brush.

5

Turn under 2" (5 cm) at the lower edge, forming the hem pocket. Fuse in place at the top of the hem pocket, using fusible web.

(Continued)

HOW TO MAKE A ROLLER SHADE
(Continued)

6

Mark a line down the center of the roller by holding the roller firmly in place on a table; lay a marker flat on the table and slide it down the length of the roller.

7

Tape the upper edge of the shade, wrong side up, along the marked line, from the inner edge of the pulley to the inner edge of the plug. Roll the shade on the roller. The wrong side of the shade will be visible on the roller, but will be covered by the valance.

8

Trim the hem stick to fit the pocket at the lower hem; slide it into the pocket. Mount the roller shade into the brackets.

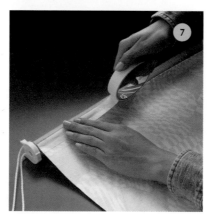

SWITCH PLATE

Holographic vinyl was glued over painted circles to turn this light switch into a stoplight.

HOW TO MAKE A HANDKERCHIEF VALANCE

1

Measure the outside width of the window frame and add 2" (5 cm) to determine the length of the mounting board, for a window with an inside-mounted roller shade. Or, if the roller shade is mounted outside the frame, add 2" (5 cm) to the measurement from bracket to bracket. Cut the mounting board.

2

Secure angle irons within 1" (2.5 cm) of each end of the mounting board, with one side aligned to the board back. Mount the board above the window frame. If the roller shade is inside-mounted, the angle irons should be just outside the frame on both sides and the board bottom should rest on the frame. If the shade is mounted outside the frame, mount the board high enough above it to clear the fully raised shade. Remove the board from the angle irons.

3

To avoid vertical seams in the valance, cut the fabric with the valance width (horizontal) running on the lengthwise grain of the fabric. The cut width of the valance is equal to the length of the mounting board plus 25" (63.5 cm). The cut length of the valance (vertical) is 32" (81.5 cm). Cut interlining the same width as the valance and 16" (40.5 cm) long.

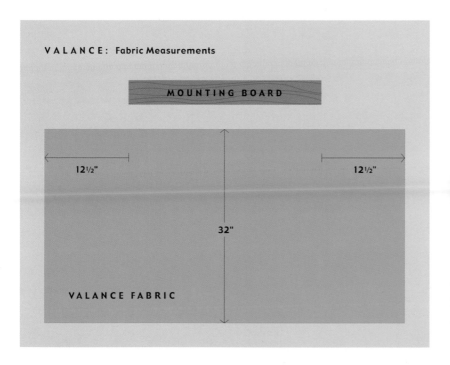

VALANCE: Fabric Measurements

MOUNTING BOARD

12½"   12½"

32"

VALANCE FABRIC

4

Place the interlining over the wrong side of the valance, aligning it to one long edge and the short ends; pin. Stitch ⅜" (1 cm) from the three outer edges.

5

Fold the fabric rectangle in half lengthwise, right sides together; pin the raw edges together. Stitch ½" (1.3 cm) seams, leaving a 10" (25.5 cm) opening along the long edge for turning the valance right side out. Trim the seam allowances diagonally at the four corners.

6

Press the seam allowances open. Turn back the seam allowances ½" (1.3 cm) along the opening, and press. Turn the valance right side out, and press. Stitch the opening closed.

7

Center the valance over the mounting board with the long stitched edge along the back of the board. The valance should extend the same distance off both ends and off the front of the board. Staple in place near the back edge.

8

Mount the valance, reattaching the board to the angle irons. Adjust the front corners of the valance to fall in gently rounded folds.

Traffic Sign Pillows

Boxy, oversized pillows shaped like traffic signs make great floor cushions or comfy backrests for quiet-time activities. An inner core of polyurethane foam is wrapped with batting for extra plumpness. Zippered closures make the covers easy to remove for cleaning.

MATERIALS

- Polyurethane foam, 4" (10 cm) thick
- Upholstery batting
- Mediumweight cotton fabrics in red and yellow, for sign backgrounds; ⅝ yd. (0.6 m) per pillow
- Black and white medium-weight cotton fabrics for boxing strips and appliqués, 60" (152.5 cm) wide; ½ yd. (0.5 m) per pillow
- Paper-backed fusible web
- Basting tape or glue stick
- 18" (46 cm) zipper

TOOLS

- Scissors or rotary cutter and mat
- Iron
- Sewing machine; zipper foot
- Electric knife or long knife with serrated blade, optional

HOW TO MAKE A SQUARE OR OCTAGONAL SIGN PILLOW

1

For square signs, cut the pillow back and front 19" (48.5 cm) square. For an octagon, cut two 19" (48.5 cm) squares. Mark 5" (12.7 cm) from each corner, draw diagonal lines connecting the marks, and trim off the corners. For a round sign, cut two 19" (48.5 cm) circles. Cut two 3" (7.5 cm) strips of fabric 19" (48.5 cm) long for the zippered section of the boxing strip. Cut a 5" (12.7 cm) boxing strip from the entire crosswise width of the fabric.

2

Enlarge patterns. Trace mirror-image letters and symbols (page 76) onto the paper backing of the fusible web. Fuse the backing to the wrong side of the appliqué fabric, following the manufacturer's directions. Cut out the appliqués.

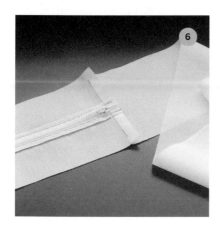

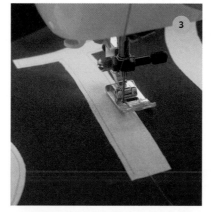

3

Fuse the appliqués to the pillow front. For a more secure attachment, stitch ⅛" (3 mm) from the edges of the appliqués.

4

Baste the zipper strips, right sides together, ½" (1.3 cm) from one long edge; finish the seam allowances separately by zigzagging or overlocking. Press the seam allowances open.

5

Secure the zipper face-down over the seam, applying basting tape or glue stick to the outer edges of the zipper tape. From the right side, stitch ¼" (6 mm) from the seam down both sides of the seam.

6

Stitch one end of the zipper strip to the boxing strip, right sides together, using ½" (1.3 cm) seam; begin and end ½" (1.3 cm) from edges and backstitch to secure.

7

Stitch the boxing strip to the pillow back, right sides together, using ½" (1.3 cm) seam; stitch with boxing strip on top. Begin 3" (7.5 cm) from the open end of the zipper strip. For square pillows, plan the end seams of the zipper strip to align to the pillow corners. Clip ⅜" (1 cm) into the boxing strip at all other corners, and pivot. Stop stitching about 6" (15 cm) from where you started.

8

Stitch the open end of the zipper strip to the boxing strip so that the boxing strip will fit the remaining space. Trim off excess boxing strip. Finish stitching strip to pillow back.

9

Clip ⅜" (1 cm) into boxing strip on open side directly across from each pivot point. Remove basting on zipper seam; open zipper. Pin pillow front to boxing strip, aligning clips to corners; stitch.

10

Turn pillow cover right side out through zipper opening. Cover the foam form with batting (page 77); insert the form into the cover and zip closed.

PILLOW APPLIQUÉS: Flag man, Stop, Railroad Crossing, & Stoplight

HOW TO MAKE A ROUND SIGN PILLOW

1

Follow steps 1 to 6 on pages 74 and 75. Staystitch a scant ½" (1.3 cm) down each side of the boxing strip. Clip up to but not through the stitching line on both sides every ½" (1.3 cm).

2

Quarter-mark the outer edge of the pillow front and back. Stitch the boxing strip to the pillow back, as in steps 7 and 8, omitting reference to corners or clipping. Stitch just inside staystitching, keeping cut edges even. Remove zipper strip basting and open zipper.

3

Pin pillow front to opposite side of boxing strip, aligning quarter marks; stitch. Finish as in step 10.

HOW TO PREPARE THE PILLOW INSERT

1

Draw a pattern for the foam that is 1" (2.5 cm) narrower than the finished size of the pillow. Have foam cut at the store or cut it yourself. Trace the pattern onto 4" (10 cm) foam, using a permanent marker. Cut foam, using an electric knife or a long knife with a serrated blade, keeping the knife blade perpendicular to the foam surface.

2

Cut two pieces of batting 2" (5 cm) larger than the pattern on all sides. Center foam over one piece of batting; place other piece on top. Whipstitch batting edges together by hand, using a sturdy thread and a long darning needle. Pinch out excess batting at corners; trim. Stitch edges together.

3

On round pillow form, ease batting fullness in as you stitch.

TRUCK TOY CHEST

Disguise a wooden toy chest as a semi cab, following the general directions for the school bus toy chest on page 54.

CHEERFUL KITES RIDE ON THE

sky-blue breeze, skittering past feathery clouds

in this daydreamer's digs. Eye-catching colors

and simple lines launch the energetic, carefree

spirit of this bedroom and the lucky kid who hangs

out here. Affordable, yet sturdy and versatile

furnishings are effortlessly fashioned from

PVC pipe and nylon canvas. In this lively escape,

imagination takes off with bright ideas for

organizing and storing a kid's treasures and trifles.

Kites & Clouds

Bold Striped Duvet Cover

Make a splashy cover for a comforter or duvet, using bold stripes of primary and secondary colors that echo the vibrant colors of classic kites. For best results, use tightly woven, washable fabrics and prewash them before cutting the pieces. The measurements given are for a twin-size duvet cover with a finished size of 68" × 88" (173 × 223.5 cm). If your child has a larger comforter, adjust the sizes of the cut pieces to get the correct finished size.

RIGHT: Ribbon streamers drawn through grommets are tied into breezy bows for a clever closure.

MATERIALS

- 2³⁄₈ yd. (2.2 m) fabric in five colors (blue, green, orange, red, and purple)
- Yellow fabric; 7 yd. (6.4 m) if 45" (115 cm) wide or 5 yd. (4.6 m) if 60" (152.5 cm) wide
- 1 yd. (0.92 m) grosgrain ribbon, ⁵⁄₈" (15 mm) wide, in each of the five colors
- Five ³⁄₈" (1 cm) grommets
- 2 yd. (1.85 m) narrow twill tape and four small plastic rings, for securing comforter inside cover
- Thread

TOOLS

- Scissors or rotary cutter and mat
- Tape measure; straightedge
- Sewing machine
- Grommet attaching tool

HOW TO MAKE A STRIPED DUVET COVER

1

Cut a lengthwise strip of each of the five colors for the top of the duvet cover, measuring 14⅝" × 82½" (37 × 209.5 cm). Stitch the strips together, using ½" (1.3 cm) seam allowances and following the color order as listed opposite. Finish seam allowances together; press seam allowances away from center.

2

Cut yellow pieces for the back 89" (226 cm) long. Use a full width of the fabric for the center and stitch partial, equal-width strips on the outer edges so the back measures 69" (175.3 cm) wide.

3

Cut a strip of yellow fabric for the front top, measuring 69" × 26½" (175.3 × 67.3 cm). Turn under and press 8" (20.5 cm) on one long edge; unfold. Turn cut edge under to fold line; press. Refold, forming 4" (10 cm) double-fold hem.

4

Make a 4" (10 cm) double-fold hem in the upper edge of striped piece. Lap yellow hem over striped hem; baste together within the ½" (1.3 cm) seam allowances at outer edges.

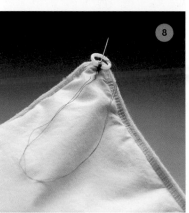

5

Insert the grommets in the center of the top hem, centered above each stripe. On each colored stripe, secure a matching ribbon directly under each grommet, stitching three times across the center of the ribbon.

6

Pin front to back, right sides together. Stitch ½" (1.3 cm) seam all around. Finish seam allowances; press open.

. . . .

HINT: To press the seam allowances open, insert a sleeve roll, hard cardboard tube, or large wooden dowel between the layers through the opening. Center the pressing aid under the seam and press.

7

Cut four 18" (46 cm) pieces of twill tape. Stitching through the strip center, securely stitch the tape to the seam allowances ½" (1.3 cm) from a corner. Repeat at each corner.

8

Securely stitch a plastic ring to each corner of the comforter. Spread out the cover, striped side down; spread the comforter over it. Tie the comforter to the cover at the corners.

9

Turn the cover right side out, encasing the comforter. Thread the ribbons through the grommets and tie into bows or knots.

Stenciled Sheets & Pillowcases

Give ordinary white or pastel sheets a custom look with kite-shaped stencils along the hems. Use a purchased kite stencil or copy the pattern and cut your own stencils; cutting a separate stencil for each color makes the actual stenciling go a little faster. You can use acrylic craft paints for stenciling on fabric; simply apply fabric medium to the paints to ensure that the finished designs will last through frequent laundering.

MATERIALS

- Stencil blanks
- Fine-point permanent marker
- Thin cardboard
- Acrylic paints in colors to match duvet cover
- Acrylic fabric medium
- Repositionable stencil adhesive
- Paper plate

TOOLS

- Craft knife and cutting mat
- Tape measure
- Disappearing fabric marker
- Foam pouncers or makeup sponges, one for each color

HOW TO MAKE A KITE STENCIL

1
Trace the kite design five times onto stencil blank, using a fine-point permanent marking pen. Allow at least a 1" (2.5 cm) margin around each design.

2
Cut out marked design, using a mat knife and working on a cutting mat. Pull knife toward you as you cut, turning the stencil, rather than the knife, to change direction.

HOW TO STENCIL THE SHEETS & PILLOWCASES

1
Launder new sheets and pillowcases to remove any sizing from the fabric; do not use fabric softener. Measure the length of the hems and mark the desired position of the designs, spacing them evenly. Using disappearing fabric marker, label the intended color for each design.

2
Apply repositionable stencil adhesive to the back of the stencil, following the manufacturer's directions. Place fabric over cardboard to prevent paint from marking through to another layer. Place the stencil on the fabric at the first mark. Press around openings with fingers.

3
Pour a small amount of paint onto a paper plate; mix in fabric medium, following manufacturer's directions.

4

Dip pouncer or makeup sponge into paint. Blot off excess on another area of the plate. Hold pouncer perpendicular to fabric, and apply paint using an up-and-down pouncing motion.

5

Lift stencil and reposition at next mark for the same color. Apply all stencils of same color before switching to another stencil and another color.

6

Allow the designs to dry 24 to 48 hours. Heat-set the designs, using a dry iron and a pressing cloth.

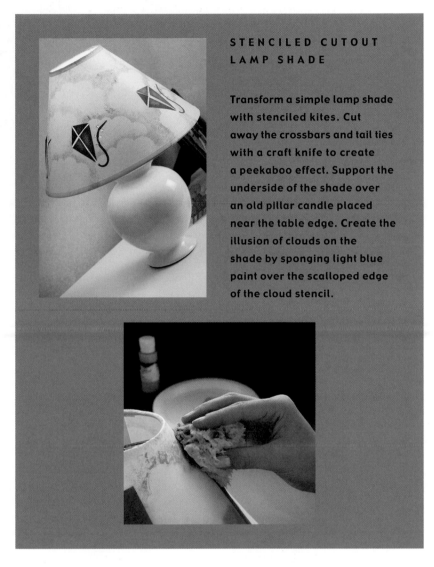

STENCILED CUTOUT LAMP SHADE

Transform a simple lamp shade with stenciled kites. Cut away the crossbars and tail ties with a craft knife to create a peekaboo effect. Support the underside of the shade over an old pillar candle placed near the table edge. Create the illusion of clouds on the shade by sponging light blue paint over the scalloped edge of the cloud stencil.

STENCILS

Table & Chairs

Make lightweight but sturdy chairs from ordinary PVC pipe and nylon canvas. Attach a wooden tabletop to wide PVC pipe legs for stable support. The set can grow with the child from toddler to preteen age simply by changing a few of the pipe pieces in the chairs and cutting longer legs for the table.

The PVC pipes fit the joints very tightly, so gluing is not necessary. The seat and back can then be removed for laundering if needed, simply by pounding the joints apart with a rubber mallet. If made of nylon canvas, the seat and back can be washed clean while still on the frame.

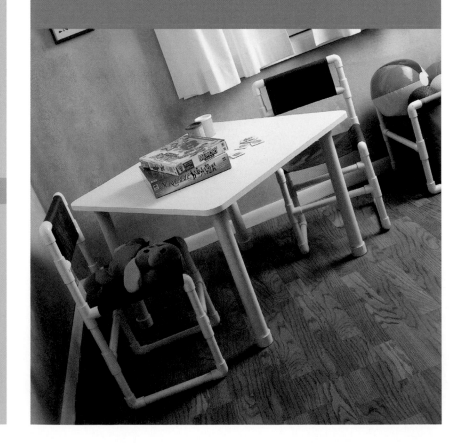

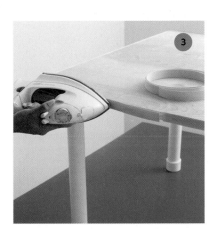
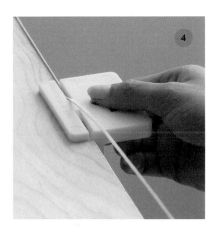

HOW TO MAKE A PINT-SIZE TABLE

1

Round the tabletop corners. Predrill three holes, evenly spaced, near the the inner edge of four end caps, using countersink bit. Place caps 1½" (3.8 cm) from table edges at each corner. Predrill shallow pilot holes in table; secure caps to table.

2

Cut 1½" (3.8 cm) PVC pipe into four table legs of desired length. Pound legs into end caps, using rubber mallet. Pound remaining end caps onto ends of table legs. Apply adhesive felt circles to end caps, if desired.

3

Sand entire tabletop until smooth. Wipe with tack cloth. Apply veneer edging to the edge of the tabletop, aligning one edge with top and allowing excess to extend toward underside. Follow manufacturer's directions.

4

Break away excess edging; sand edging lightly. Paint or stain and finish tabletop as desired.

AS KIDS GROW, table legs can be replaced inexpensively, and the ten PVC pieces that make up the chair legs and lower part of the chair back can be replaced with slightly longer ones. As a general rule, there should be a space of 6" to 10" (15 to 25.5 cm) between the chair seat and the tabletop. Use the chart below to adjust the height of the table and chairs to suit the size of your kids.

AGE	2-3	4-5	6-7	8-9
STANDARD SEAT HEIGHT	10" (25.5 cm)	12" (30.5 cm)	14" (35.5 cm)	16" (40.5 cm)
EIGHT SHORT PIECES IN CHAIR LEGS	3" (7.5 cm)	4" (10 cm)	5" (12.7 cm)	6" (15 cm)
TWO SHORT PIECES IN LOWER CHAIR BACK	4" (10 cm)	4" (10 cm)	5" (12.7 cm)	6" (15 cm)
LENGTH OF TABLE LEGS	16" (40.5 cm)	18" (46 cm)	20" (51 cm)	22" (56 cm)

2

HOW TO MAKE A PINT-SIZE CHAIR

1
Cut fabric for the chair seat 12½" × 22½" (31.8 × 57 cm); cut the chair back 12" × 15" (30.5 × 38 cm). Press a ¼" (6 mm) double-fold hem in the long ends of each piece; stitch.

2
Fold under short ends of seat ½" (1.3 cm); press. Fold under again 3" (7.5 cm). Stitch along folded edge, forming casing. Stitch again ¼" (6 mm) from first stitching. Reinforce stitches, using short narrow zigzag at ends.

3
Pin short ends of back, right sides together. Stitch ½" (1.3 m) seam. Trim seam allowances, and finish seam allowances together. Turn right side out.

4
Clean pipes, using acetone and a soft cloth; wear rubber gloves. Carefully measure and mark these cut lengths for the pieces as indicated in the diagram: eight 10½" (26.7 cm), eight 12" (30.5 cm), and twenty-four 4" (10 cm). Cut pieces, using PVC pipe cutter for a clean, even cut. Or use a hacksaw and sand the edges smooth. These measurements are for a chair seat height of 12" (30.5 cm). See the suggestions and chart on page 85 to adjust the height.

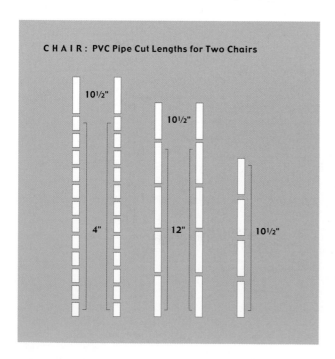

CHAIR: PVC Pipe Cut Lengths for Two Chairs

10½"   10½"   12"   10½"   4"

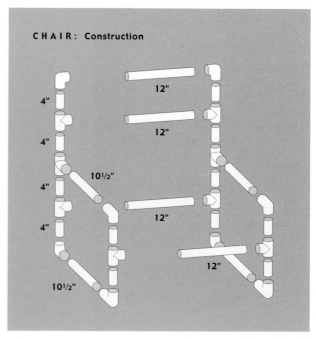

CHAIR: Construction

4"   12"   12"   4"   4"   10½"   4"   12"   4"   12"   10½"

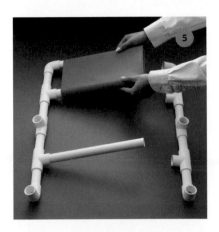

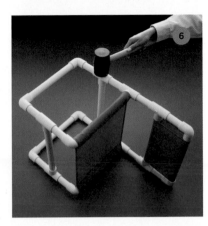

5

Connect elbows, tee fittings, and pipe pieces to make one side of chair. Insert 10½" (26.7 cm) pipes through seat casings before connecting to front elbow and back tee fitting. Repeat for opposite side of chair.

6

Insert two 12" (30.5 cm) cross pieces through chair back. Connect chair sides with cross pieces at elbows and tee fittings. Pound all pipes securely into fittings, using a rubber mallet.

PAINTED FAN BLADES & DRESSER DRAWER KNOBS

Paint the blades of a ceiling fan with bright acrylic paints that echo the colors of the bed. Repeat the colors on furniture drawer pulls, too. For cleaning ease, use semigloss paints on wood surfaces. They won't attract smudgy little finger-prints and the slick finish wipes clean easily.

MATERIALS

- Six 60" (152.5 cm) lengths of 1" (2.5 cm) PVC pipe
- Four tee fittings for 1" (2.5 cm) PVC pipe
- Four elbows for 1" (2.5 cm) PVC pipe
- Four rubber end caps to fit 1" (2.5 cm) PVC pipe
- 2½ yd. (2.3 m) nylon canvas
- ⅓ yd (0.32 m) nylon canvas in each of three colors, for pockets
- 68" (173 cm) Velcro, ¾" (2 cm) wide
- Thread
- Eight bolts, nuts, and washers for attaching headboard and footboard to bed frame

TOOLS

- PVC pipe cutter or hacksaw and sandpaper
- Acetone and clean cloth; rubber gloves
- Rubber mallet
- Drill and drill bits
- Screwdriver
- Sewing machine

Headboard & Footboard

Bright nylon canvas is stretched over lightweight PVC pipe frames to make an economical headboard and footboard for the bed. Both upper frames are made with the same pipe measurements; the footboard has shorter legs than the headboard. Three handy, oversized storage pockets on the headboard are great places to store nighttime necessities, like tissues, a small flashlight, or books. Repeated on the footboard, the pockets are large enough for storing stuffed animals or other small toys. Velcro® closures make it easy to remove the canvas covers for occasional laundering.

    The measurements given are for a twin bed with a distance of 37" (94 cm) between bolts on the bed frame. If your child has a larger bed, measure the distance between bolts on the frame and adjust the horizontal pipe lengths and the fabric widths accordingly. Add a pocket or widen the three pockets to fill the space.

HOW TO MAKE A HEADBOARD & FOOTBOARD

1
Clean pipes, using acetone and a soft cloth; wear rubber gloves. Carefully measure and mark these cut lengths for the pieces as indicated in the diagram: four 35½" (90.3 cm) crossbars; four pipe lengths 16½" (41.8 cm) long for sides; two pipe lengths 25" (63.5 cm) long for the headboard legs; two pipe lengths 16½" (41.8 cm) long for the footboard legs. Cut pieces, using a PVC pipe cutter for a clean, even cut. Or use a hacksaw and sand the edges smooth.

(Continued)

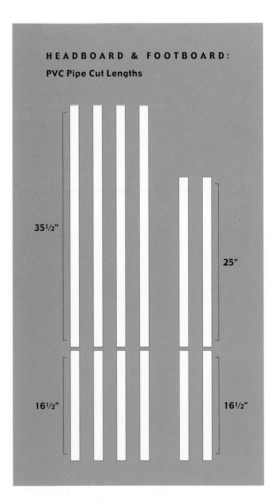

HEADBOARD & FOOTBOARD:
PVC Pipe Cut Lengths

35½"

25"

16½"   16½"

HOW TO MAKE A HEADBOARD & FOOTBOARD
(Continued)

2

Connect the elbows, crossbars, side pieces, tee fittings, and legs to make the frames, following the diagram. Pound pieces together securely, using a rubber mallet.

3

Cut two fabric center pieces for the headboard and the footboard 43½" × 35½" (110.5 × 90.3 cm). Cut four side pieces 6½" × 16" (16.3 × 40.5 cm). Cut six pockets 12" × 12" (30.5 × 30.5 cm).

4

Fold a pocket in half sideways, right sides together. Stitch 1" (2.5 cm) from fold, 1½" (3.8 cm) from lower edge; backstitch at ends. Open pleat; press flat. Repeat for each pocket.

5

Press under pocket top hem 1" (2.5 cm); topstitch in place. Press under ½" (1.3 cm) on bottom and sides, mitering corners. Repeat for each pocket.

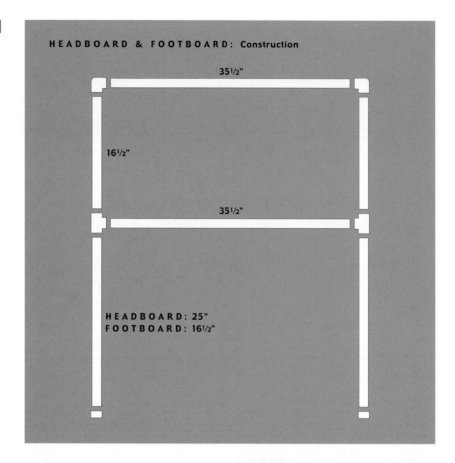

HEADBOARD & FOOTBOARD: Construction

35½"

16½"

35½"

HEADBOARD: 25"
FOOTBOARD: 16½"

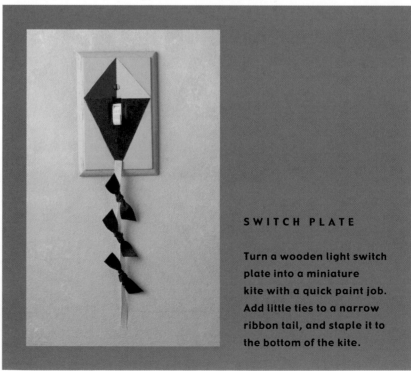

SWITCH PLATE

Turn a wooden light switch plate into a miniature kite with a quick paint job. Add little ties to a narrow ribbon tail, and staple it to the bottom of the kite.

6

Pin three pockets, evenly spaced, on headboard center piece, with outer edges of outer pockets 2½" (6.5 cm) from sides and 5½" (14 cm) from bottom edge. Topstitch in place ⅛" (3 mm) from outer folds. Backstitch at upper edges.

7

Fold headboard center piece in half. Mark sides 2¾" (7 cm) and 17" (43 cm) below center fold on front and back. Unfold.

8

Fold under ½" (1.3 cm) on short ends of side pieces; topstitch ⅜" (1 cm) from fold. Pin one long edge of side piece to center front, right sides together, aligning ends to marked points. Stitch ½" (1.3 cm) seam. Pin and stitch opposite edge to back. Repeat for remaining side piece.

9

Press seams toward center, pressing under remaining side edges ½" (1.3 cm). Topstitch ⅜" (1 cm) from fold.

10

Press under ½" (1.3 cm) on bottom edge closest to pockets. Pin and stitch hook side of Velcro over raw edge, with one side of tape aligned to fold. Press ½" (1.3 cm) to right side on remaining bottom edge; stitch loop tape over raw edge.

11

Repeat steps 6 to 10 for the footboard. Slip the covers over the frames. Overlap and seal the bottom edges.

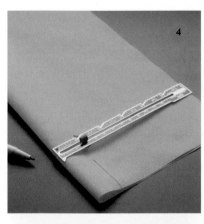

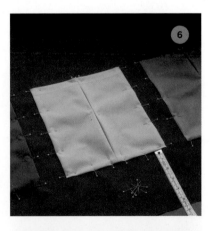

Kite Bulletin Board

Make a colorful, lightweight bulletin board
by covering foam core board with fabrics to match
the duvet cover. Add a jaunty ribbon tail with
colorful ties.

MATERIALS

- 24" × 30" (61 × 76 cm) piece
  of foam core board, ¹/₂"
  (1.3 cm) thick
- Fabrics in four colors
- 1 yd. (0.92 m) yellow grosgrain
  ribbon, 1¹/₂" (3.8 cm) wide
- 12" (30.5 cm) grosgrain
  ribbon, 1¹/₂" (3.8 cm) wide,
  in three colors for tail ties
- Spray adhesive
- Adhesive hangers

TOOLS

- Scissors
- Craft knife and cutting mat
- Thin bladed instrument, such
  as a butter knife

HOW TO MAKE A KITE BULLETIN BOARD

BULLETIN BOARD: Measurements

10"

33"

11½"   11½"

23"

23"

1

Draw a vertical 33" (84 cm) line on a large sheet of paper; cross the line 10" (25.5 cm) from the top with a horizontal 23" (58.5 cm) line, extending equal distances to each side. Connect the ends of the lines to make a kite pattern. Trace the kite on the foam-core board. Cut out the kite, using a long-bladed craft knife and a cutting mat.

2

Draw the intersecting lines on the kite front. Cut on the marked lines, taking care to cut only half-way through the board; mark a guide line on the knife blade for accuracy. Cut 1" (2.5 cm) grooves completely through each outer corner.

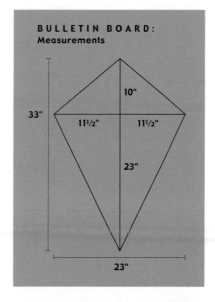

3

Trace the kite on a large sheet of paper. Draw the dividing lines and cut the sections apart to make patterns. Cut a fabric piece for each section ¼" (6 mm) larger on the two inner edges and 1½" (3.8 cm) larger on the outer edge.

4

Spray the wrong side of a fabric piece with adhesive. Place the fabric over the kite section, overlapping the inner lines ¼" (6 mm). Using a thin, flat blade, push the fabric edge down into the precut grooves.

5

Wrap excess fabric around the outer edge to the kite back. Tuck excess into 1" (2.5 cm) grooves at corners.

6

Repeat steps 4 and 5 for each section. Cut ribbon pieces diagonally. Glue one end of tail to back side of kite. Attach ties evenly spaced. Attach adhesive hangers to kite back.

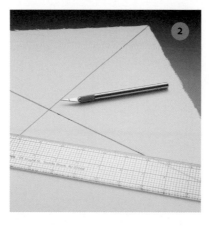

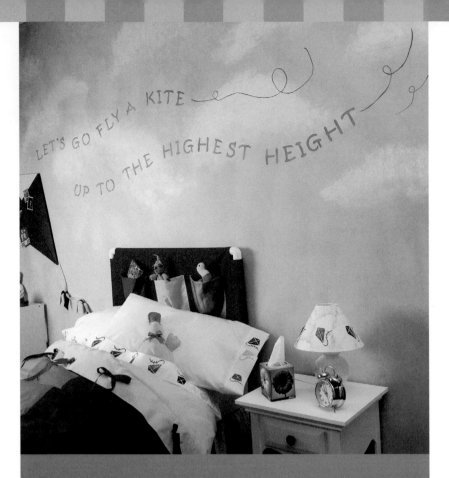

LET'S GO FLY A KITE UP TO THE HIGHEST HEIGHT

Partly Cloudy Painted Wall

Slightly textured, sky-blue walls are painted easily and quickly, using a dual, deep pile paint roller and two shades of blue paint. The roller, paint tray, small paintbrush, and touch-up pad are available in a kit manufactured by The Woolie™, Inc. As the paint is applied, the colors blend together softly, creating a color-washed look in half the time of traditional color-washing techniques. Once the sky is dry, wispy clouds are added in a matter of minutes, using an easy-as-pie technique. As a finishing touch, the first line from a Mary Poppins song is stenciled onto the wall, "Let's go fly a kite!"

HOW TO PAINT A PARTLY CLOUDY WALL

1
Mask off all the woodwork in the room, using painter's masking tape. Cover the floor and furniture with dropcloths.

2
Pour the two blue paints into their separate sections of the paint tray. Load the dual roller with the two colors, covering the rollers completely; remove excess paint on the tray ramp.

HINT: Select the two blue paint colors from the same monochromatic paint sample strip. Find the blue shade you have in mind, and then purchase paint in the two blue shades on either side of that shade, one lighter and one darker. To create a more blustery day, choose shades that are farther away from your starting point.

MATERIALS

- Painter's masking tape
- Two blue shades of satin-finish, latex paint
- White and gray latex paints
- Paint glaze

TOOLS

- Dual roller tray
- 9" (23 cm) paint roller frame
- Dual, deep-pile roller cover
- Two 1" (2.5 cm) paintbrushes or foam applicators
- 4" (10 cm) foam applicator
- Sea sponge or small wool blending pad

3

Apply the paint to a 4' × 4' (1.23 × 1.23 m) wall area in short strokes, alternating in all directions. The more you roll through the colors, the more they will blend together. Work as close as possible to any corners or edges.

4

Load a small paintbrush with both colors. Apply the paint up to any corners or edging, working in sections of about 2' (0.6 m) at a time. Blend the colors together by patting with a damp sea sponge or small wool blending pad, blending the touch-up area into the rolled area.

5

Repeat steps 2 to 4, working adjacent areas around the entire room. Allow the paint to dry thoroughly.

HINT: If you are right-handed, start with the upper half wall in the upper right corner. Paint the lower half next. Then, work your way around the room to the left, always painting the upper half first. This helps you avoid smearing paint if you accidentally lean into the wall as you work. Reverse the direction if you are left-handed.

6

In separate containers, mix small amounts of white and gray paint with paint glaze, following the glaze manufacturer's proportion guidelines. To paint a cloud, apply a short arch of white paint glaze to the wall, using a 4" (10 cm) foam applicator. Apply a shorter gray arch under the white one, using a 1" (2.5 cm) foam applicator.

7

Pat a damp sea sponge or a small blending pad over the arches, softening the glaze into a cloud-like, translucent form; blend the gray into the white to create natural-looking shadows.

8

Repeat steps 6 and 7 for each cloud, varying the sizes and shapes and scattering them randomly over the upper third of the walls.

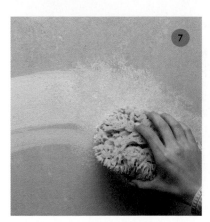

Toy Hamper

Stuffed animals, building blocks, board games, or dolls are tucked away neatly in a colorful toy hamper that is easy and economical to make. Three nylon canvas bags are suspended in a sturdy PVC pipe frame that can be disassembled for laundering.

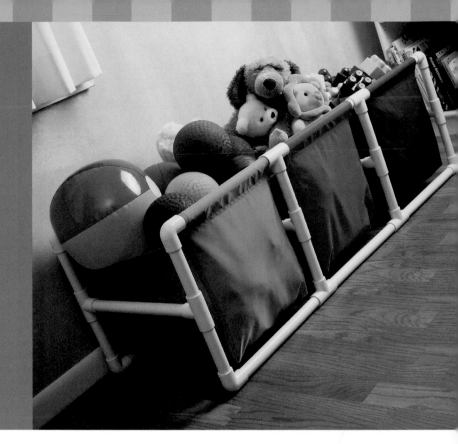

MATERIALS

- ⁷/₈ yd. nylon canvas, 60" (152.5 cm) wide, in each of three colors
- Thread
- Six 60" (152.5 cm) lengths of ³/₄" (2 cm) PVC pipe
- Eight elbows for ³/₄" (2 cm) pipe
- Sixteen tee fittings for ³/₄" (2 cm) pipe

TOOLS

- Sewing machine
- PVC pipe cutter or hacksaw and sandpaper
- Acetone and clean cloth; rubber gloves
- Rubber mallet

HOW TO MAKE A TOY HAMPER

1
For each bag, cut one piece of canvas 51" × 13" (129.5 × 33 cm); cut two pieces 16½" × 14½" (41.8 × 36.8 cm).

2
Fold under 1" (2.5 cm) twice, forming a double-fold hem on one long side of each small rectangle. Stitch along inner fold and again ¼" (6 mm) away from first stitching line. Mark the centers of the ends opposite the hems.

3
Mark a casing line 5½" (14 cm) from the short ends of the large rectangles. Mark the centers of the long edges; make ³/₈" (1 cm) clips into the seam allowance 7¾" (19.7 cm) on each side of center on both long edges.

HAMPER: PVC Pipe Cut Lengths

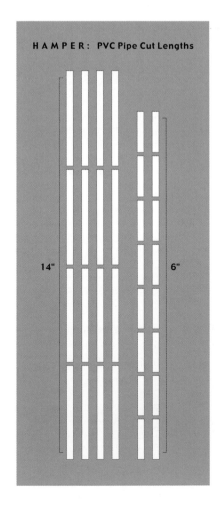

14"   6"

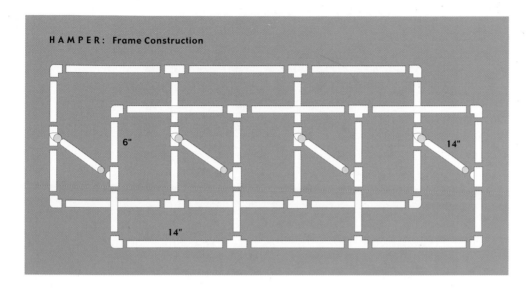

HAMPER: Frame Construction

6"

14"

14"

4

Pin the small rectangle to the large rectangle, right sides together, aligning center marks. Align upper hemmed edge to casing lines, and align clips to corners. Stitch ½" (1.3 cm) seams, pivoting at corners and backstitching at ends. Repeat for opposite side.

5

Press seam allowances toward long piece; press under ½" (1.3 cm) on sides of casing extensions. Topstitch next to and ¼" (6 mm) from folds and seams.

6

Turn under ½" (1.3 cm) on short ends of extensions; align folds to casing lines. Stitch on folds; stitch again ¼" (6 mm) away from first stitching line.

7

Repeat steps 4 to 6 for remaining bags. Clean pipes, using acetone and a soft cloth; wear rubber gloves. Carefully measure and mark these cut lengths for the pieces as indicated in the diagram: sixteen 14" (35.5 cm) pieces; sixteen 6" (15 cm). Cut pieces, using a PVC pipe cutter for a clean, even cut. Or use a hacksaw and sand the edges smooth.

8

Slide a 14" (35.5 cm) pipe length into each casing at the tops of the bags. Connect the elbows, tee fittings, and pipe pieces to make the frames, following the diagram. Pound pieces together securely, using a rubber mallet.

Coat Tree

If you're looking for a place to hang jackets and other kid gear, take a walk down the plumbing aisle. It's amazing what you can create with a little imagination and some PVC pipe—this coat tree, for example. Even the base is fashioned from a plumbing fitting.

MATERIALS

- 10" × 10" (25.5 × 25.5 cm) board, ³⁄₄" (2 cm) thick
- Primer; paint
- One 60" (152.5 cm) length of 2" (5 cm) PVC pipe
- End cap for 2" (5 cm) pipe
- PVC bell trap drain, 6 × 6, 2 × 3 fit
- Five 10" (25.5 cm) lengths of ³⁄₄" (2 cm) PVC pipe
- Ten end caps for ³⁄₄" (2 cm) pipe
- Wood screws

TOOLS

- Acetone and clean cloth; rubber gloves
- Sandpaper; tack cloth
- Paintbrush
- PVC pipe cutter or hacksaw and sandpaper
- Drill and drill bits; 1" (2.5 cm) hole bit
- Grinding bit
- Rubber mallet

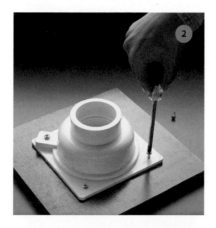

HOW TO MAKE
A PVC COAT TREE

1

Sand the wooden base; wipe with tack
cloth. Apply primer; allow to dry. Apply
paint; allow to dry.

2

Clean the pipes and bell trap, using
acetone and a soft cloth; wear rubber
gloves. Center the bell trap on the base.
Drill pilot holes in four corners;
insert screws.

3

On one end of large pipe, mark points
dividing the circle into eighths.
Lay pipe on flat surface. Lay pencil
on surface with tip aligned to one
point. Draw line down the pipe
about 28" (71 cm) by sliding pencil
along surface; keep pipe stationary.
Repeat for each of first four
marked points.

4

Mark points on first line 2½" (6.5 cm)
and 26½" (67.3 cm) from the end.
On the next line, mark a point 8½"
(21.8 cm) from the end. On the
third line, mark a point 14½" (36.8 cm)
from the end. On the fourth
line, mark a point 20½" (52.3 cm)
from the end.

5

Using the hole bit, drill through the
pipe at the first mark, keeping the bit
perpendicular to the pipe. Drill through
until small center bit comes through
other side. Repeat at each mark.

6

Turn pipe over and drill holes in
opposite side at holes created by center
bit. Enlarge each hole slightly, using
grinding bit, until small pipe fits hole
snugly. Insert a small pipe through
each set of holes, centering it in the large
pipe. Place end caps on small pipes.

7

Insert bottom of large pipe into bell trap.
Pound in place firmly, using rubber mallet.

HINT: Secure the pipe in a vise
with the marked points squarely in the
center. This will free both hands to
guide the drill.

Ribbon-tab Curtains

Suspend crisp white window curtains from a pole with colorful ribbon tabs that are laced through grommets in the curtains. Purchase washable fabric, and preshrink it before cutting by washing and drying in the same water and dryer temperatures you intend to use for laundering the finished curtains. If privacy or light control are needed, install a simple white roller shade or mini blind behind the curtains.

HINT: As an alternative, purchase ready-made curtain panels and add the grommets and ties to the upper casing or hem. Space the grommets 8" to 10" (20.5 to 25.5 cm) apart.

MATERIALS

- White cotton or cotton blend fabric, 45" (115 cm) wide; amount determined in step 1 (allow extra for shrinkage).
- ³/₈" (1 cm) grommets, five per curtain panel
- Thread
- 1 yd. (0.92 m) grosgrain ribbon, ⁵/₈" (15 mm) wide, in each of five colors to match duvet cover
- Wood pole and brackets; screws

TOOLS

- Carpenter's square
- Sewing machine
- Iron
- Grommet setting tool
- Drill and bits; screwdriver

HOW TO MAKE RIBBON-TAB CURTAINS

1

Measure the window from the top of the frame to the bottom of the apron. Add 12" (30.5 cm) to determine the cut length of each curtain panel. Use one full width of fabric for each panel; make two panels for each window. Cut the panels, using a carpenter's square for accuracy.

2

Press under 8" (20.5 cm) at the bottom of the panel. Unfold and turn the cut edge back, aligning it to the pressed foldline; press the outer fold. Refold the hem, and stitch along the inner fold, forming a 4" (10 cm) double-fold hem.

3

Cut off the selvages evenly. Press and stitch 1" (2.5 cm) double-fold hems in the sides.

4

Press a 1½" (3.8 cm) double-fold hem in the panel top. Unfold fabric at the corners. Trim out the excess fabric from the inner layer, trimming to within ⅜" (1 cm) of the fold.

5

Refold the upper hem, and stitch. Mark placement for the grommets in the top hem, with the end marks ¾" (2 cm) from the sides. Space the remaining three marks evenly.

6

Attach the grommets at the marks, following the manufacturer's directions. Center the grommets between the fold and the stitching line.

7

Install the wood pole 3" to 4" (7.5 to 10 cm) above the window frame. Wrap ribbon over the pole; insert both ends through the grommet from the back. Tie ribbons in bows or knots so that the top hem of the curtain is just above the window frame. Cut ribbon tails to desired length.

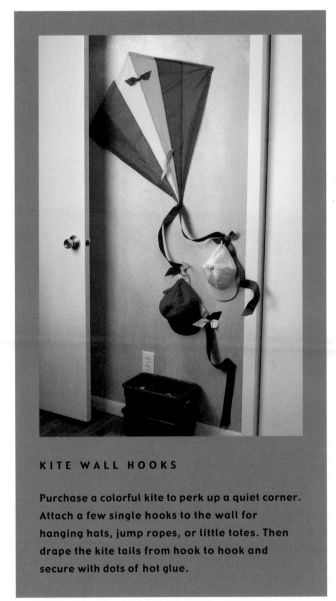

KITE WALL HOOKS

Purchase a colorful kite to perk up a quiet corner. Attach a few single hooks to the wall for hanging hats, jump ropes, or little totes. Then drape the kite tails from hook to hook and secure with dots of hot glue.

SOME KIDS ARE JUST MEANT TO

live in the woods; they're captivated by the call

of the wild and the adventure of sleeping out

under the stars. In a bedroom that offers all the

amenities of a cozy campsite, your little

nature lover can live such a dream every night,

while sleeping safe and sound just a stone's

throw away from you. The bedroom is designed

with plenty of convenience and versatility

for you and your camper, without blowing the

"roughing-it" smoke screen.

Camper's Paradise

Walls

By day, these walls are Nature's playland, beckoning a kid to take a romp through the meadow or climb a nearby tree. Apparently, a friendly bear wandered through the campsite, too! At night, the stars twinkle in the sky and the fireflies hover in the grass. All this magic is created with paint, imagination, and some simple techniques.

MATERIALS

- Satin latex paint in sky blue and grass green
- Craft paints in various colors
- Glow-in-the-dark paint
- Glow-in-the-dark star stickers, optional
- Purchased stencils for stars, bugs, and butterflies
- Stencil blanks for cutting paw prints
- Repositionable stencil adhesive

TOOLS

- Paint rollers; paint trays
- Paintbrushes
- Foam pouncers for stenciling bugs and butterflies
- Craft knife and cutting mat
- Small foam roller for stenciling paw prints

HOW TO PAINT THE CAMPSITE WALLS

1
Mark off a gently rolling horizon line partway up the wall. Paint the wall blue above the line; allow to dry. Paint the wall green below the line. Paint random spiky strokes with a paintbrush along the dividing line to resemble grass. Allow to dry.

2
Apply repositionable stencil adhesive to bug and butterfly stencil backs; position on wall. Stencil bugs and butterflies, using various colors of craft paint, applying the paint with foam pouncers.

3
Stencil bugs randomly in the grass and sky, using glow-in-the-dark paint to resemble fireflies. Stencil glow-in-the-dark stars high on the wall. Mark star locations for a few constellations on the ceiling, and stencil a glow-in-the-dark star at each mark. Substitute glow-in-the-dark star stickers, if desired.

4
Enlarge paw print pattern, opposite. Transfer to a stencil blank, and cut out. Apply repositionable stencil adhesive to the stencil back. Stencil a trail of paw prints around the room along the lower part of the wall; apply the paint, using a foam roller.

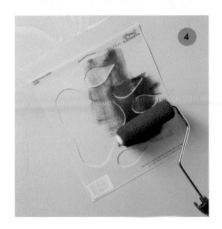

FRIENDLY FIRS

A few miniature lifelike pine trees add a realistic look to the room. Cuddly stuffed bears are found clutching the branches of the taller trees.

STENCIL:
Enlarge
200%

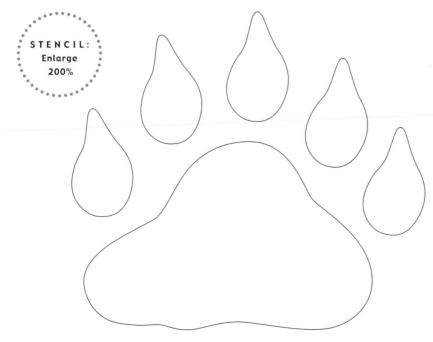

HINT: What's a campsite without a few hefty rocks? Cushion their flat sides with self-adhesive felt.

MATERIALS

- 1¼ yd. (1.15 m) fake fur
- 1¼ yd. (1.15 m) polyester felt
- 1¼ yd. (1.15 m) rug backing
- Temporary spray adhesive for fabric
- Thread

TOOLS

- Scissors
- Rotary cutter with wave blade, cutting mat
- Sewing machine

Bear Rug

Soft fur underfoot adds a comfortable touch to your little camper's wooded hangout. Look for fur and felt that are machine washable.

HOW TO MAKE A BEAR RUG

1

Enlarge the pattern; transfer the inner line to the back of the fur. Cut out the bear, using shears; cut only through the backing, avoiding the fur fibers.

2

Preshrink the felt by laundering. Cut the felt, following the outer line of the pattern, using a rotary cutter with a wave blade.

3

Apply temporary spray adhesive to the wrong side of the fur. Center fur on right side of felt; pin around outer edge. Zigzag around outer edge, pushing fur fibers away from presser foot as you stitch.

4

Cut rug backing the same size as the fur pattern. Place rug backing on the floor. Center the bear rug over it.

HINT: There are nonslip rug backings suitable for carpets and hard floors. Be sure to read the label and purchase the right kind for your child's room.

BEAR: Left half

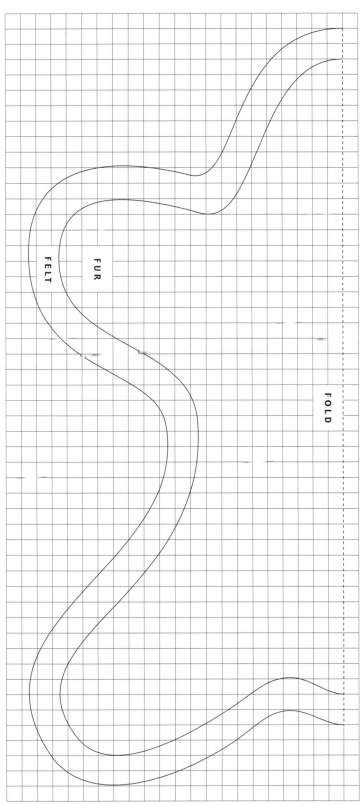

FELT

FUR

FOLD

RUG
PATTERN:
1 Square=1"
(2.5 cm)

COOL STORAGE

Inexpensive plastic coolers make handy storage chests and can double as extra seating or a surface for playing games. The covers do not lock, but for extra safety around little tykes, remove the drain plugs.

Rustic Shelf

Brackets and pegs made from real branches give these shelves an outdoor look. The shelf and backboard are cut from 1 × 6 pine. Any branches that are relatively straight and free of rot or disease are suitable for the brackets and pegs.

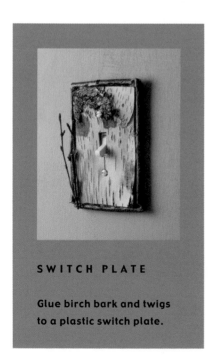

SWITCH PLATE

Glue birch bark and twigs to a plastic switch plate.

ABOVE: Follow the directions on page 111 to revamp a mirror frame.

MATERIALS

- Two 1 × 6 pine boards in desired length
- Small branches, about 1½" (3.8 cm) in diameter, for support brackets
- Small branches, about ½" (1.3 cm) in diameter for pegs
- 8 × 1⅝" (4 cm) drywall screws; brads and nail set
- Paint or stain
- Clear acrylic finish
- Picture hanger with screws
- Rubber or cork bumpers

TOOLS

- Jigsaw or circular saw; crosscut saw
- Drill and drill bits
- Hammer, chisel, chain, awl, and 100-grit sandpaper, for distressing wood

HOW TO MAKE A RUSTIC PEG SHELF

1
Cut shelf board and backboard to the desired length.

2
Distress the wood, if desired, by pounding randomly with a hammer, chisel, chain, or awl. Chisel the edges roughly and round off edges, using 100-grit sandpaper.

3
Predrill screw holes 1" (2.5 cm) from the upper edges of the backboard, using ³⁄₃₂" drill bit; position holes about 2" (5 cm) from ends and at 6" to 8" (15 to 20.5 cm) intervals. Mark corresponding positions for screw holes on back edge shelf; predrill holes. Secure shelf to backboard with drywall screws.

4

Paint or stain the shelf as desired; allow to dry.

5

Cut a strip of paper to the approximate width of the branch to be used for the support bracket. Place the end of the shelf on the paper as shown; position the paper as desired for the placement of the branch. Mark the paper along the inside edges of wood boards for angle of cuts; label top and bottom of bracket.

6

Cut paper on marked lines; place on branch, and mark angle of cuts. Cut branch on marked lines. Repeat for additional brackets.

7

Position bracket on shelf; mark. Predrill hole through backboard for wood screw. Predrill hole through shelf for brad, using drill bit that is slightly smaller than brad diameter. Holding bracket in place, insert screw from back of backboard; insert brad from top of shelf board. Repeat for additional brackets.

8

Cut 3" (7.5 cm) pegs from the smaller branches. Predrill screw holes for pegs through backboard, 2" (5 cm) from lower edge. Predrill holes in peg ends. Secure pegs to backboard with drywall screws.

9

Countersink brads on top of shelf, using nail set. Fill holes with putty to match stain or touch up with paint. Apply clear acrylic sealer to shelf.

10

Secure hangers near upper corners of shelf back. Secure bumpers at lower corners, layering bumpers as needed to make shelf hang level.

Twig-letter Name Plaque

It only takes a few minutes to turn a handful of twigs into a clever name plaque. Look for a weathered board or distress a purchased plaque for the base.

HOW TO MAKE A TWIG-LETTER NAME PLAQUE

1
Cut the baseboard to the desired size. Distress the wood as on page 108, step 2, if desired. Lightly mark the letters on the board with pencil.

2
Cut twigs for the letters, using a pruner. Glue twigs in place with hot glue.

3
Decorate the plaque with pine cones, acorns or gnarled twigs as desired.

4
Drill holes ½" (1.3 cm) from the upper corners. String twine through the holes, knots the ends, and hang the plaque.

Nature Frames

With scraps of bark
and tiny pinecones, recycle
a few old picture frames or
decorate unfinished
frames from the craft store.
Use them to showcase
a collection of your child's
favorite animal photos or
pictures taken on a family
camping trip.

MATERIALS

- Picture frames with relatively flat surfaces
- Birch bark or other types of tree bark, collected from firewood or fallen trees
- Twigs, small pinecones, acorns, lichens

TOOLS

- Utility knife; wood chisel or putty knife
- Heavy-duty scissors
- Hot glue gun and glue sticks

HOW TO MAKE NATURE FRAMES

1
Remove bark from log by cutting it lengthwise with a utility knife and prying it away with a wood chisel or putty knife. Flatten slightly curled bark by steaming it with an iron and pressing it between boards until dry.

2
Break or cut the bark into small pieces or cut an opening in a large piece of bark the same size as the frame opening, using a utility knife.

3
Secure bark to frame front, using hot glue gun. Embellish the frame with small twigs, pinecones, acorns, or lichens.

Whittlin' Away Grow Chart

The growth progress of your little one is marked with notches carved on a tree trunk. Standing watch over the campground scene is a friendly bear cub clinging to the branch.

MATERIALS

- Relatively straight tree branch, 2" to 3" (5 to 7.5 cm) in diameter, 5' to 6' (1.58 to 1.85 m) tall
- Additional branches 1" (2.5 cm) in diameter for braces
- 12" (30.5 cm) square of ¼" (6 mm) plywood for base
- Wood stain; clear acrylic finish
- Wood screws
- Artificial tree branches
- Small stuffed bear

TOOLS

- Saw
- Miter box
- Hammer, chisel, chain, awl, sand paper, for distressing wood, optional
- Drill and bits
- Hot glue gun and glue sticks
- Needle and thread

HOW TO MAKE A WHITTLIN' AWAY GROW CHART

1

Distress and stain the baseboard as on page 108, if desired. Cut four 6" (15 cm) supports from 1" (2.5 cm) diameter branches; cut the ends at 45° angles.

2

Make sure the large tree branch is cut square across the bottom. Remove any smaller branches. Predrill a hole up into the center of the branch, perfectly perpendicular to the cut; predrill another hole through the center of the base. Secure the branch to the base with a long flathead wood screw.

3

Position the angled braces on four sides of the branch. Secure upper ends to branch, using small wood screws. Secure braces to base with flathead wood screws inserted from the underside of the base.

4

Drill holes in upper area of branch, angling slightly upward. Insert artificial branches of leaves; secure with hot glue. Perch a stuffed bear on one of the branches, with its limbs circling the large branch. Secure by hand-tacking the paws together, if necessary.

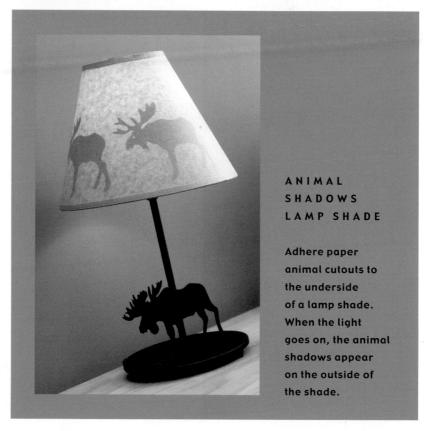

ANIMAL SHADOWS LAMP SHADE

Adhere paper animal cutouts to the underside of a lamp shade. When the light goes on, the animal shadows appear on the outside of the shade.

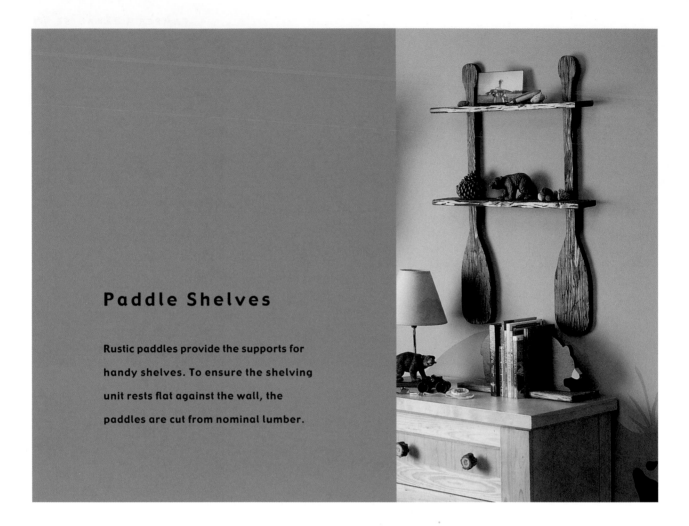

Paddle Shelves

Rustic paddles provide the supports for handy shelves. To ensure the shelving unit rests flat against the wall, the paddles are cut from nominal lumber.

MATERIALS

- 6' (1.85 m) 1 × 6 pine
- 4' (1.27 m) 1 × 4 pine
- Wood stain; clear acrylic finish
- Four 2" (5 cm) drywall screws
- Two picture hangers with screws
- Rubber or cork bumpers

TOOLS

- Jigsaw
- Drill, drill bits
- Screwdriver
- Hammer, chisel, chain, awl, sandpaper for distressing wood

HOW TO MAKE PADDLE SHELVES

1
Enlarge paddle pattern. Trace pattern twice onto 1 × 6 board; cut out paddles. Cut two 24" (61 cm) shelves from 1 × 4 wood.

2
Distress wood as on page 108, if desired. Stain and finish all surfaces.

3
Drill pilot holes through paddle centers 6" (15 cm) from the top and 16" (40.5 cm) from the bottom. Drill pilot holes into centers of shelf back edges 4" (10 cm) from each end, making sure holes are perpendicular to surface.

4
Attach shelves to paddles, inserting wood screws from paddle backs. Secure hangers near tops of paddle backs. Secure bumpers to back of paddle blades to keep shelves level.

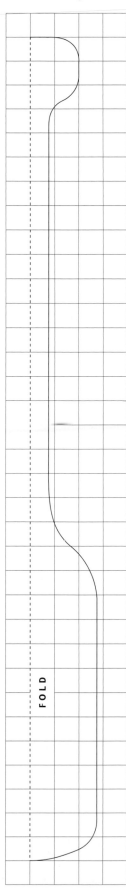

FOLD

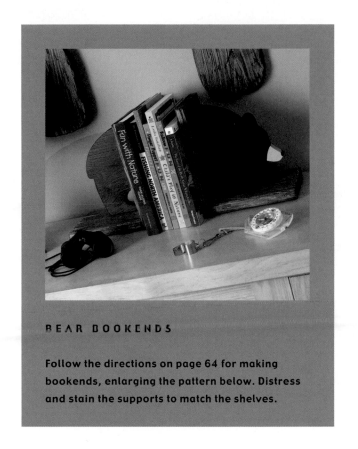

BEAR BOOKENDS

Follow the directions on page 64 for making bookends, enlarging the pattern below. Distress and stain the supports to match the shelves.

BEAR BOOKEND: Back & Front

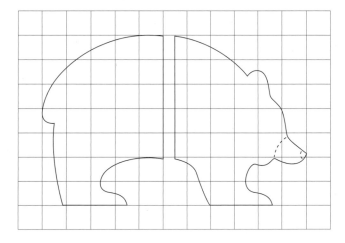

PATTERNS:
1 Square=1"
(2.5 cm)

HOW TO MAKE A BEAR TRACK COVERLET

1

Copy the bear paw print pattern on page 105. Cut paw print appliqués from brown fleece. Place the comforter on the bed. Position appliqués on the comforter to look as if a bear walked across it; secure with temporary spray adhesive.

2

Edgestitch around all the appliqué pieces.

Bear Tracks Bedding Set

When your little camper feels like sleeping in a real bed, this cozy fleece bedding set will ensure a snug, warm retreat. It looks like that friendly bear found it tempting, too. Fleece is such a user-friendly fabric; it doesn't ravel, it is easily laundered, and its comfort factor is off the charts! We chose to make our bear sham for a queen size bed pillow, which fits the width of a twin bed better than a standard size.

HOW TO MAKE THE FRINGED BED SKIRT

1

Place a fitted sheet over the box spring. Using water-soluble marking pen, mark the sheet ½" (1.3 cm) in from the upper edge on the sides and foot.

2

Measure from the marked line to the floor. Cut three strips of fleece this width in lengths 2" (5 cm) longer than sides and foot of the bed, cut on the lengthwise grain.

3

Place masking tape 6" (15 cm) from one long edge of each strip. Cut slits for fringe from the edge to the tape, every ¾" (2 cm). Remove tape.

4

Pin the strips to the fitted sheet, overlapping the marked line ¼" (6 mm); overlap the strips at the foot corners. Remove the sheet from the box spring. Stitch the skirt to the sheet, stitching ¼" (6 mm) from edge over the marked line. Replace the sheet on the box spring.

PUP TENT

Set up a small pup tent in a corner to create a cozy hideaway for reading, napping, or other quiet-time activities. Look for one that does not require staking to stand up. Equip the tent with a sleeping bag and small fringed fleece pillows made similar to the pillow sham on page 118. Hang a battery-operated tent light inside.

HOW TO MAKE
THE BEAR SHAM

1

Measure the pillow width and length from seam to seam. Cut a piece of fleece for the sham top 10" (25.5 cm) wider and longer than the pillow. Cut a piece of fleece for the sham bottom 13" (33 cm) wider (side to side) and 10" (25.5 cm) longer (top to bottom) than the pillow.

2

Cut the back in half from top to bottom, to create an opening for inserting the pillow. Cut two pieces of grosgrain ribbon the same length as the cut edges. Seal the ribbon ends with liquid fray preventer. Pin the ribbon to the right side of these cut edges. Stitch along both edges of the ribbon to reinforce the edges.

3

Cut the stars, bear, and moon appliqués from yellow, tan, and white fleece, using the patterns. Spray appliqué backs with temporary spray adhesive; position in center of sham top, following the pattern. Edgestitch around appliqués.

4

Mark a stitching line around the sham top 5" (12.7 cm) from the cut edge, using narrow masking tape. Overlap the back pieces 3" (7.5 cm). Place the sham front over the back, wrong sides together; pin around the outer edge, just outside the tape. Stitch around the sham, guiding the presser foot along the edge of the tape. Remove pins.

PILLOW SHAM: Stars, Moon, & Bear Appliqués

5

Mark the tape every ¾" (2 cm) for cutting the fringe; begin in the center, so cuts can be planned to avoid cutting into ribbon. Adjust fringe width toward corners as needed. Cut fringe, using a straightedge as a guide; cut to within ⅛" (3 mm) of stitching line. Remove tape.

SMALL PILLOWS

Make 16" (40.5 cm) toss pillows with removable covers, following the bear sham directions. Make these changes in measurements: cut fronts 22" (56 cm) square; cut backs 22" × 25" (56 × 63.5 cm), for pillows with 3" (7.5 cm) fringe. Insert 16" (40.5 cm) pillow forms.

APPLIQUÉ
PATTERNS:
1 Square=1"
(2.5 cm)

SMALL PILLOWS: Tree, Small Tree, & Moose Appliqués

Twig Headboard

An authentic twig headboard adds to the woodsy character of the bedroom. Building with real tree limbs is easier than you think, especially when making something as uncomplicated as this headboard. It doesn't have to be sturdy enough to bear any weight, and you don't have to worry about pieces fitting plumb. Cut fresh twigs and branches that are fairly smooth and sturdy or look for dried branches, perhaps at a local brush recycling center. Branches with about 2" (5 cm) diameter work well for the two upright posts; the cross pieces can be ¹/₂" to 1" (1.3 to 2.5 cm) in diameter.

HINT: For the safety of little ones, build the headboard with spaces too small to fit a head through. If you want to make a twig footboard, secure vertical branches so ends are even with the top crossbar rather than poking up above it.

MATERIALS

- Craft paper
- Freshly cut twigs and branches
- Galvanized flathead nails
- Wood sealer or clear acrylic finish
- Twine
- Carriage bolts, washers, and cap nuts

TOOLS

- Pruners
- Saw
- Drill and bits
- Hammer

HOW TO MAKE A TWIG HEADBOARD

1

Determine the desired height, length, and width of the headboard. On a large sheet of craft paper, over a sturdy work surface, draw two parallel lines for side posts, perpendicular to a baseline. Cut two 2" (5 cm) diameter branches the desired length for side posts; place in position.

2

Cut two 1" (2.5 cm) diameter cross pieces about 4" (10 cm) longer than the distance between the posts. Position one cross piece at about the height of the mattress top; position the other 2" (5 cm) from the top. Predrill holes through the cross pieces into the posts; secure with nails.

3

Cut several small branches 4" (10 cm) longer than the distance between the cross pieces. Position them as desired behind the cross pieces; predrill holes and secure with nails.

4

Lash the intersections with twine, crisscrossing several times over the front, covering the nails; knot securely in the back.

5

Allow the headboard to cure for at least one month. Then apply interior wood sealer or clear acrylic finish.

6

Stand the headboard behind the bed frame and mark for the position of the carriage bolts. Drill holes for the bolts; secure the headboard to the frame.

TRUNK-CHUNK FURNITURE KNOBS

Fashion husky knobs by cutting 1" (2.5 cm) slices of a tree branch, about 2" (5 cm) in diameter. Predrill holes halfway into the back of the slices and secure them to the drawers with screws inserted from the inside of the drawer. Use small wooden craft spools as spacers between the knobs and the drawer front. Apply a clear sealer.

Tent Flap Curtains

Cleverly designed tent flap curtains unzip down the center and fold back like a real tent. Mounted on a 1 × 2 board, the curtain is installed just above and outside the window frame. Depending on the length of the window, you can use a sleeping bag zipper or an upholstery zipper or purchase heavy-duty zipper by the yard.

MATERIALS

- Nylon fabric
- Zipper with heavy plastic or metal teeth, slightly longer than length of window; separating zipper acceptable but not necessary
- Basting tape
- Thread
- 1½ yd. (1.4 m) grosgrain ribbon, ⅝" (15 mm) wide
- 1 × 2 mounting board, cut 2" (5 cm) longer than outside width of window frame
- Glue, optional
- Four 1" (2 cm) angle irons; screws
- 3" (7.5 cm) Velcro®
- Fishing bobber; snap swivel

TOOLS

- Scissors
- Sewing machine
- Iron
- Staple gun
- Drill; screwdriver

HOW TO MAKE TENT FLAP CURTAINS

1

Cut fabric to cover the mounting board, with width of fabric equal to circumference of board plus 1" (2. 5 cm) and length equal to board length plus 3½" (9 cm). Wrap board like a gift, with edges overlapping on one wide side; secure with staples or glue.

2

Secure angle irons within 1" (2.5 cm) of each end of the mounting board, with one side aligned to the board back. Mount the board above the window frame. Measure for the finished curtain length from the top of the mounting board to the bottom of the frame. Leaving the angle irons on the wall, remove the board.

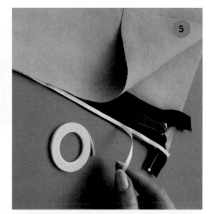

3

Cut two curtain panels, each equal in width to the mounting board length plus twice the depth plus ½" (1.3 cm). The cut length is equal to the desired finished length plus the mounting board depth, plus 1" (2.5 cm).

4

Pin the zipper face-down on the right side of one lengthwise edge, so the zipper top is at the panel bottom. Turn the zipper tape ends toward the wrong side of the zipper at an angle; pin.

5

Fold the panel in half lengthwise, right sides together, aligning the lengthwise edges. Secure with double-stick basting tape along the outer edge, with zipper encased between the fabric layers; pin layers together at top and bottom. Stitch ⅜" (1 cm) from the lengthwise edges; stitch ½" (1.3 cm) from the top and bottom edges, leaving a 10" (25.5 cm) opening for turning along the top.

6

Trim corners diagonally. Finish the zipper seam allowances together with the zipper tape edge. Turn the panel right side out; press.

7

Repeat steps 4 to 6 for the opposite panel. In step 5, the entire finished panel will be encased between the layers of the unfinished panel. It is pulled back out through the opening when the second panel is turned right side out.

8

Stitch the openings closed. Cut two 27" (68.5 cm) pieces of ribbon. Fold a piece in half, and pin to the outer edge of one panel, one-third of the distance from the bottom, with one ribbon tail on each side of the fabric. Stitch a 1½" (3.8 cm) strip of Velcro loop tape to the edge of the wrong side of the panel, over the ribbon. Repeat for the other panel.

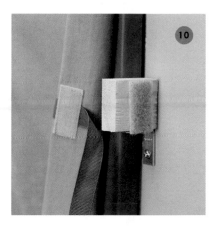

9

Staple the curtain to the mounting board, aligning the upper edge of the curtain to the back edge of the board; wrap outer edges around board ends, forming miters at corners.

10

Mount the curtain, reattaching the board to the angle irons. Cut two 1½" (3.8 cm) pieces of 1 × 2 board; staple a 1½" (3.8 cm) strip of Velcro hook tape to one wide side of each piece. Using angle irons, mount the wood pieces on each side of the window frame, aligning the Velcro strips.

11

Attach a round bobber to the zipper tab with a snap swivel. To open the curtain, unzip the panels and tie them back.

Firefly Night Light

This lantern-shaped bug cage, made by Coleman®, is recommended as a home for fireflies or other insects a kid might capture. We have outfitted it with a string of mini lights to turn it into a handy night light.

Portable, kid-size nylon camp chairs and an aluminum camp table are perfect gear for playing board games or sharing snacks.

MATERIALS

- Firefly Lantern™ by Coleman®
- String of 20 white mini lights

TOOLS

- Drill and drill bits
- Nippers

HOW TO MAKE A FIREFLY NIGHT LIGHT

1

Remove the base cap, revealing the secret compartment. Drill a hole through the top of the base and the bottom of the cage cap.

2

Carefully feed the light string through the hole and into the cage. Reach in through the cage top to distribute the lights evenly.

3

Cut a small notch in the edge of the base rim and another in the edge of the base cap. Replace the base cap, aligning the openings and feeding the wire out through them.

TRUNK-SLICE CLOCK

Unfinished pine tree trunk slices are available at craft stores in various sizes. With the use of a wood-burning pen and a clock movement, we have turned this one into a backwoods timepiece. A chunk of wood, cut at a slight angle, is glued to the lower back to make the clock stand upright.

Index

Sources

Fabric Traditions
1350 Broadway Suite 2106
New York, NY 10018
www.fabrictraditions.com
(map fabric panel, p. 52)

HTC, Inc.
103 Eisenhower Parkway
Roseland, NJ 07068
www.htc-inc.net
888-618-2555
(Fuse-A-Shade roller shade kits, pp. 44 & 70)

Walnut Hollow Farm, Inc.
1409 State Road 23
Dodgeville, WI 53533
www.walnuthollow.com
800-950-5101
(clock movements, woodcraft products,
woodburning kits)